More Tales from Baseball's Golden Age

Gene Fehler

Sports Publishing LLC.
www.SportsPublishingLLC.com

Director of Production: Susan M. Moyer
Book design/senior project manager: Jennifer Polson
Dustjacket design: Joseph T. Brumleve

Photos courtesy of Brace Photo
ISBN: 1-58261-481-4

SPORTS PUBLISHING, L.L.C.
804 North Neil Street
Champaign, IL 61820

Visit our website at www.sportspublishingllc.com

In memory of my dad, Franklin Fehler,
who would have liked this book

ACKNOWLEDGMENTS

M y deepest thanks once again to the players who so gener-ously took the time to speak with me and share with me their stories. Without their kindness and enthusiasm and love of the game there could have been no Golden Age of Baseball, nor could this book have been written.

To the late Mike Schacht, editor of *Fan* magazine, where some of the pieces about Ted Williams originally appeared.

To Hazel Fehler, my mom, who has always given me encouragement.

To John and Lew, who shared baseball dreams in our Golden Age years in Thomson, Illinois.

To my mother-in-law, Charlotte Eggert.

To Andy and Tim, Jacquelyn and Mireille, Jan, Rita, and Rhonda.

And, most of all, to Polly, with love.

CONTENTS

PREFACE

In *Tales from Baseball's Golden Age,* we heard the voices of Cal Abrams, Johnny Berardino, Jimmy Bloodworth, Ray Boone, Tommy Byrne, Andy Carey, Bubba Church, Jerry Coleman, Chuck Diering, Sonny Dixon, Bobby Doerr, Jim Dyck, Ferris Fain, Don Ferrarese, Tom Ferrick, Bob Friend, Ned Garver, Joe Ginsberg, Randy Gumpert, Dick Hall, Gail Harris, Billy Hitchcock, Art Houtteman, Sid Hudson, Ernie Johnson, Spider Jorgensen, Ralph Kiner, Nellie King, Johnny Klippstein, Bob Kuzava, Max Lanier, Bob Lennon, Don Liddle, Danny Litwhiler, Marty Marion, Tim McCarver, Cal McLish, Bob Oldis, Milt Pappas, Herb Plews, J. W. Porter, Bill Renna, Mike Sandlock, Carl Scheib, Charlie Silvera, Sibby Sisti, Frank Sullivan, Wayne Terwilliger, Frank Thomas, Bobby Thomson, Virgil Trucks, Bill Virdon, Wally Westlake, Gene Woodling, Al Zarilla, and Gus Zernial.

They shared memories about Hank Bauer, Yogi Berra, Enos Slaughter, Johnny Mize, Phil Rizzuto, Mickey Mantle, Bill Dickey, Henry Aaron, Don Larsen, Whitey Ford, Don Newcombe, Jim Bunning, Vic Raschi, Allie Reynolds, Ted Williams, Sal Maglie, Jocko Conlin, Jackie Robinson, Joe DiMaggio, Lefty Grove, Cecil Travis, Hank Majeski, Eddie Lopat, Gil McDougald, Stan Musial, Chief Bender, Harry Brecheen, Joe Cronin, Satchel Paige, Rogers Hornsby, Jimmy Piersall, Mickey Vernon, Pete Runnels, Billy Martin, Dick Donovan, Billy Gardner, Connie Mack, Harvey Haddix, Branch Rickey, Hoyt Wilhelm, Paul Richards, Brooks Robinson, Gene Mauch, Dusty Rhodes, Jimmy Foxx, Fred Haney, Duke Snider, Willie Mays, Birdie Tebbetts, Pepper Martin, Chuck

Klein, Ewell Blackwell, Alex Grammas, Pedro Ramos, Eddie Yost, Warren Spahn, John Lindell, Elmer Valo, Johnny Hopp, Eddie Waitkus, Frank Howard, Don Zimmer, Eddie Stanky, Bob Porterfield, Hal Newhouser, and many more.

To fans of the Golden Age each of these names might bring back a personal memory.

Here in *More Tales from Baseball's Golden Age* are still more players with new tales to tell, more names, more memories.

Cal Abrams

Eight years (1949-56)
Born March 2, 1924 BL TL 6'0" 185 lbs.
Positions: Outfield, 440; 1B, 4
Brooklyn Dodgers, Cincinnati Reds, Pittsburgh Pirates,
Baltimore Orioles, Chicago White Sox

G	BA	AB	H	2B	3B	HR	R	RBI	BB	SO	SB	FA
567	.269	1611	433	64	19	32	257	138	304	90	12	.977

*C*al's being thrown out at home in the last of the ninth inning at Brooklyn in 1950 remains a key moment in baseball history. His run would have forced a playoff. Instead, the Phillies won the game, and the pennant, in the 10th inning on Dick Sisler's home run. In four full minor league seasons (1946-49), Cal hit .331, .345, .337, and .336, scoring over 100 runs each season. In 1953, he hit .286 with 15 home runs in 119 games for Pittsburgh. In 1954, he hit .293 in 115 games for Baltimore. He was involved in the 1952 trade that sent Gus Bell from Pittsburgh to the Reds. In 1954, he was traded to Baltimore for Dick Littlefield. In 1955, he went to the White Sox for infielder Bobby Adams.

'50 N.L. Pennant

We were down a game to the Phillies in 1950 going into the last game of the season. If we win, we have a playoff. We were playing at Brooklyn, and we came up to bat in the last of the ninth tied. I led off with a walk. Reese got a bunt single. I'm on second with nobody out with what would be the winning run. Roberts was pitching. Lopata gave him the sign for a pick-off play at second, but Roberts missed the sign. Richie Ashburn came running in to back up second, but Roberts pitched to the plate and Snider hit a line drive past me. At his normal position, Ashburn couldn't have thrown the ball all the way to the plate. Milton Stock, the third-base coach was waving his arm and yelling, "go, go, go"—then at the last moment, he saw Ashburn in shallow and had his hand up to his mouth and his other arm up and I thought, "What kind of a sign is that? I've never seen one like that before."

But it was too late to stop. Lopata was 15 feet up the line with the ball, waiting. I ran in to him and tried to knock the ball out of his hand, but I couldn't. Then Furillo popped out and Hodges lined out to left. If I'd stayed at third, I'd have scored on Hodges' ball to left and we'd have won the pennant. The papers made me out to be a goat at first.

It was a disappointment not winning the pennant, but one good thing came out of that play for me personally. This play, and my role in it, wouldn't have been talked about for all these years if I'd have scored.

Jackie's Compliment

The Dodgers traded me to Cincinnati in 1952. I was in right field in my first game against the Dodgers. I made it a point to study people, and I knew how all the Dodgers played the game.

Jackie Robinson always rounded first base hard; he could stop on a dime, but he was always ready to go to second on a bobble.

So Jackie hit a line drive to right. I caught it on the hop and threw it to Kluszewski at first. If he'd been looking, he'd have been able to tag Jackie out at first, but he was looking at the bag to make sure Jackie didn't miss it. My throw to Klu hit him right in the chest. It didn't even faze him; that's how strong he was.

When Jackie went back to first, he turned toward me in right and smiled. That was his way of complimenting me on making a good play.

Three Brooklyn Managers

I played for three managers with the Brooklyn Dodgers: Leo Durocher, Burt Shotton, and Charlie Dressen. Of the three of them, the one who knew baseball most was Leo the Lip, Leo Durocher. But he was a very tough man; he came from a very rough neighborhood, and he was a scowler and a screamer. He knew his ballplayers, and he knew how he could get the best out of them.

And then, just the opposite, like day from night, they put in Burt Shotton, who was a kindly old gentleman. *[Shotton was 63 and hadn't managed in the big leagues for 14 years. He led the Dodgers to pennants in 1947 and 1949.]* He sat in the dugout without putting on a uniform. It reminded me of the old John McGraw and the owner of the Philadelphia ballclub, Connie Mack.

And then third, but not last, was Charlie Dressen, who I always called the First Person Singular. He always said, "I, I, I." "I know this, I know that." So what we used to do in the clubhouse when we had our meetings, we always used to sit on the foot lockers and around him when we discussed the opposing team and who was playing, and we put our hands into fists. And every time he mentioned the word "I," the first person would raise one finger, and we kept on going around the room counting each other's fingers, how many times he said "I." He would say to Carl Erskine, who was going to pitch for the day, "We're playing Philadelphia, and this new rookie pitcher, anybody know him? Or "This heavy hitter they just got from the minors, anybody know him?" And everybody said no, they don't.

He said, "Well, I know—let me tell you what I know—I know this, I know that when a man comes up from the minor leagues, I'll bet any amount of money he can't hit the curve ball." And every time he said "I," we'd keep our fingers going. Finally, one time, he saw what was going on, but he didn't understand it, and he said, "What the hell are you guys doing with those fingers going up in the air?"

The Loyalty of Brooklyn Fans

At Baltimore the fans were great, in Pittsburgh the fans were super, but there will never be a fan like the Brooklyn Dodgers. The Brooklyn Dodger ballpark, Ebbets Field, was so small behind home plate that while you were hitting you could talk to people in the stands. You could have running conversations, and that's what made it a close-knit family-like operation. The fans respected you, and they loved you. Even if we lost 10 straight games in a row, they would still fill that ballpark. Even today, these people keep sending fan mail to all the Brooklyn Dodgers. It's a wonderful, wonderful thing. It will never die. Not the Brooklyn Dodgers. Not them.

Johnny Berardino

Eleven years (1939-42, 46-52)
Born May 1, 1917 BR TR 5'11 1/2" 175 lbs.
Positions: 2B, 453; SS, 266; 3B, 91; 1B, 26; OF, 1
St. Louis Browns, Cleveland Indians, Pittsburgh Pirates

G	BA	AB	H	2B	3B	HR	R	RBI	BB	SO	SB	FA
912	.249	3028	755	167	23	36	334	387	284	268	27	.960

*B*erardino entered the University of Southern California on a football scholarship, intending to play quarterback, but played baseball instead. He signed with the St. Louis Browns after his second year at USC, where he led the conference in hitting. Signed as a second baseman, he played primarily shortstop with the Browns in 1940 and '41. In 1940, he hit 16 home runs and drove in 95 runs. In 1941, he dropped to five home runs, yet drove in 89 runs. He spent from 1943-45 in the military. He had a unique career in that in his last three seasons he played for the same three teams twice each, in the same order: Browns, Indians, Pirates, Browns, Indians, Pirates. He was traded to the Indians in 1947 and played 50 games for the Indians in their World Championship season in 1948. A child actor, he returned to acting after his career

*ended, taking the role of Dr. Steve Hardy on the television soap
opera General Hospital in 1963 and playing it for more than 30
years.*

Making the Folks Proud

I loved Satchel Paige. He was such a dear fellow. Probably the
greatest pitcher who ever lived. We played an exhibition game, the
Bob Feller All-Stars against the Satchel Paige All-Stars here in Wrigley
Field in Los Angeles, my hometown. The Paige All-Stars traveled
on one plane, a DC-3, and Bob Feller's All-Star team had their own
DC-3. So we did a 30-day tour of the country. We were up here in
L.A. and we drew a big crowd, of course my folks were there—and
the first time I went up to bat against Satchel he laid one in there
and I hit it out of the ballpark. He was talking to me as I'm circling
the bases. He says, "I laid that one in there 'cause your folks are
here, Johnny. The next time you come up you ain't going to get a
loud foul." Sure enough, he was right, he struck me out three straight
times after that. Yeah, he let me have one for my folks.

The Movies or Washington?

After the 1947 season, I was doing a movie out here in Hollywood when I got traded from St. Louis, who had finished eighth,
to Washington, who had finished seventh, and I thought, "No point
in doing that." So I decided I was going to quit baseball, and that
raised a lot of hullabaloo and the deal was called.

Then Bill Veeck flew out here and said, "Look, I'd like to sign
you up for Cleveland, I'll double your salary." He made the offer so

wonderful, so lucrative, that I couldn't turn it down. My leg was bothering me and I was thinking about pursuing a movie career. Had Bill Veeck not interceded, that's what would have happened. So I don't know that he did me a great service; I wasted five years after 1947 playing utility mostly.

But then when I reflect on it, I think, "I wouldn't have a World Series ring if it wasn't for him."

I was with three different teams twice, and that was ironic. I kept going back and forth to the same three teams, twice. *[Browns to Indians to Pirates to Browns to Indians to Pirates.]*

The Offers

When I finished my sophomore year at the University of Southern California and led the conference in hitting, our coach called me in and said, "It's my duty to let you know that some major league scouts have come to see me and they want to make some offers for your services. But we'd like to see you finish college."

I said, "What do you mean? Offers for what?"

He says, "Well, they'd like to sign you up to a major league contract."

And I said, "You're talking about money?"

And he said, "Yes. The Detroit Tigers will offer you ten thousand. The Red Sox will offer you eight thousand."

And my God, my face turned ashen. I said, "Coach, I've already signed with somebody."

He said, "Who?"

I said, "The St. Louis Browns."

And he said, "Did they give you a bonus?"

I said, "No."

But you see, the scout was such a fast talker, he had come to my house and fast-talked me and my dad, both of us who didn't know anything about bonuses or anything like that, and he said, "Son, I'll guarantee you you'll be in the big leagues in two years."

Well, he was right about that, but that's all he was right about. I didn't get any money from them.

Jimmy Bloodworth

Eleven years (1937, 39-43, 46-47, 49-51)
Born July 26, 1917   BR   TR   5'11"   180 lbs.
Positions: 2B, 867; 1B, 53; 3B, 22; OF, 5; SS, 3
Washington Senators, Detroit Tigers, Pittsburgh Pirates,
Cincinnati Reds, Philadelphia Phillies

G	BA	AB	H	2B	3B	HR	R	RBI	BB	SO	SB	FA
1002	.248	3519	874	160	20	62	347	453	200	407	19	.976

Bloodworth batted .289 for the Senators in 1939, his first full season. A steady performer, he played in over 100 games during his next four seasons, batting between .241 and .245 each year. He hit a career-high 13 home runs in 1942. After two years in the military, he played in more than 100 games only once, hitting .261 in 134 games for the Reds in 1949, including an eight for 14 mark as a pinch hitter. He was traded with Doc Cramer to the Tigers in 1941 for Frank Croucher and Bruce Campbell.

Jimmy Bloodworth

Mind Games

Jimmy Foxx caught quite a bit *[Foxx, a Hall of Fame first baseman, caught 109 games during his 20-year career]*, and a lot of times I'd go up to bat and he'd say, "Well, what do you want to hit, kid? Call what you want so you can really get yourself a hit."

Well, if I'd tell him I wanted a fast ball, he'd throw me a curve. The next time he'd say, "I'll give you what you want this time."

I said, "Throw me a curve."

Then he'd throw me a curve and I wasn't looking for it. He'd do things to you like that.

Old Bobo

It's a funny thing about old Bobo Newsom—he knew you, everybody was his friend, and his arm must have been made out of rubber. He could throw that ball, and he threw it any time they wanted him to pitch. I don't think he ever had a sore arm or even thought about one. *[In 20 big league seasons, Newsom played for 17 clubs, won 211 games, and lost 222. He started at least 27 games in 14 straight seasons.]*

He was just a big old friendly bear of a fella, had legs on him like oak trees, was strong as a bull. He'd talk to you when you'd go up there to hit. He'd say, "You think you're going to get a hit? I'm going to strike you out." Things like that. He was always in the ballgame.

Milt Bolling

Seven years (1952-58)
Born Aug. 9, 1930   BR   TR   6'1"   177 lbs.
Positions: SS, 305; 2B, 55; 3B, 18
Boston Red Sox, Washington Senators, Detroit Tigers

G	BA	AB	H	2B	3B	HR	R	RBI	BB	SO	SB	FA
400	.241	1161	280	50	7	19	127	94	115	188	5	.954

In Bolling's first full season in the big leagues, he hit .263 in 109 games at shortstop for the Red Sox, completing an infield that had Gernert at first, Gardner at second, and Kell at third. He hit .249 in 113 games the following year, but injuries limited him to part-time duty his last four seasons. He played five minor league seasons before joining Boston in 1952. In 1957, he was traded to Washington with Russ Kemmerer and Faye Throneberry for Dean Stone and Bob Chakales. Milt's brother Frank, a second baseman, joined the Tigers in 1954 and had a 12-year big league career, the first 11 of those years as a regular.

First Game

I played in the first major league game I ever saw. I'd come up from Birmingham and joined the club in Detroit, and it was early September, I guess. I don't remember the exact date. So I was sitting there watching—Trucks had thrown two no-hitters that year— he didn't have a good year that year, but he'd thrown two no-hitters *[a 5-19 record, but one of only four pitchers to pitch two no-hitters in one year]*. This was 1952.

I was just sitting on the bench watching the game, and about the sixth inning, Boudreau got ticked off at everybody. The players had already gone out on the field, like Johnny Lipon and George Kell and Hoot Evers and all those guys that had played at Detroit and had been traded from Detroit. *[All three had been traded from Detroit to Boston earlier that year.]* So he told Gene Stephens and me and a few other guys to get in the game. Well, I had my hat off and I'd forgotten where I'd laid my glove.

Anyway I went out there and Lipon said a few cuss words to me, 'cause he was mad because I was showing him up at the place where he had played for a long time *[he had played six years at Detroit, the previous four as their regular shortstop]*.

I said, "Look, the man sent me out here."

The first time up, I faced Trucks, and he walked me. The second time up, in the ninth, I just luckily got one off the fists and it blooped over the shortstop's head, a broken-bat single.

I thought Lou Boudreau was an excellent manager. He was trying to get people to chart pitches and things which nobody did much back in those days. Because I played shortstop and he played shortstop, he helped me a lot on little things that you need to know about the game. We were bringing in a lot of young guys to play, and some of the older guys who were shunned aside or being made to ride the bench awhile didn't particularly like him. But the younger guys did because he gave us a chance to play.

Ray Boone

Thirteen years (1948-60)
Born July 27, 1923   BR TR 6' 172 lbs.
Positions: 3B, 510; SS, 464; 1B, 285; 2B, 1
Cleveland Indians, Detroit Tigers, Chicago White Sox,
Kansas City Athletics, Milwaukee Braves, Boston Red Sox

G	BA	AB	H	2B	3B	HR	R	RBI	BB	SO	SB	FA
1373	.275	4589	1260	162	46	151	645	737	608	463	21	.966

Boone was named to two All-Star teams, 1954 and 1956. He led the American League with 116 RBIs in 1955. A catcher in his first minor league season at Wausau, he batted .306. As a shortstop in the Texas League, he was hitting .355 in 87 games when he was called up to Cleveland to replace Lou Boudreau on the pennant-winning Indians. He hit .301 for Cleveland in 1950 and .308 for Detroit in 1956. He had 20 or more home runs for four straight years. Ray is the father of major league catcher and manager, Bob, and grandfather of major league players, Bret and Aaron.

Three Generations

[The Boones are the first three-generation family in the big leagues—Ray, son Bob, grandsons Aaron and Bret]. Just because you belong to a father who is a big league ballplayer, unless you love the game, you're not going to make it. And consequently from day one, Bob and his brother had the love for baseball, as Bob's boys right now do. I'm proud that we're the first three-generation family in the big leagues. I never ever thought too much about that as being such a big deal until it really happened, and then you kind of think, "You know, that's never been done before." And whenever you're number one in something, whether or not you're the best ever, you're still the first.

A Lifetime in Baseball

How does one sum up a lifetime in baseball—51 years as player and scout—in a few words?

Do I start with my first year in pro ball, 1942, as a catcher for Wausau?

Maybe I should begin with that awesome moment when I saw Yankee Stadium and Joe DiMaggio for the first time—a kid's dream comes true.

Or my first time at bat in Yankee Stadium and hearing my name over the P.A.

Or the sadness at seeing a lot of my teammates sent back to the minor leagues—the joy of seeing my son and grandsons play in the majors.

I wonder why it is that from all that happened during my 13 years in the big leagues, the single moment that comes to mind first is not one of my home runs—not a game-winning hit—not any great catch I made. No, the moment that leaps out at me is the eighth inning of Bob Feller's third no-hitter, back in 1951, with me at shortstop. I made an error with two outs to keep the inning alive, prayed the next hitter would pop out.

He did.

Fifty-one years in baseball. So much to try to fit into a few words.

Ted Williams' Last Home Run

The greatest hitter is Ted Williams, there's no doubt about that. Period. He was born here in San Diego as I was, so I saw Ted a lot as a kid. When Ted used to talk on hitting, he would mesmerize me. He would put me in a trance, just to watch him hit.

When we put in the shift against him, I'd come over from third base and play almost behind second. The shortstop would play second, and the second baseman would go play short right field. There were several balls that the short right fielder or the shortstop or the second baseman would pick up and throw Ted out at first. He reacted like he always did, just nonchalant about it, just go about his business. Of course, I've always said it would be nice to not worry about that base hit because you know you're going to get one next time up.

Ted hit his 500th home run in Cleveland. Around the sixth or seventh inning he hit one right down the line and the umpire called it foul. Rudy York, our first-base coach, was jumping up and down, arguing and everything. Ted went halfway down and just turned around and came back. The very next pitch he hit the same thing, but only further in for a home run.

And then I saw him homer his last time at bat in Boston in 1960. All the fans knew that this was going to be the last time they saw Williams hit, so when he came out they gave him a standing ovation. I'm sitting on the bench and I know he's going to homer. When he hit it, that place just went bananas, they're throwing cushions on the field and everything. Ted went up to the clubhouse because he was through for the day.

Finally the officials and umpires, came over and asked Pinky Higgins, our manager, "You're going to have to bring Williams back out here and take a bow, 'cause we're never going to get this game started." So he had to call up and get Ted to come back out, take his hat off, or whatever, so we could resume playing.

So that's the way to bow out in the big leagues. Hit a home run, then have them beg you to come out so they can get the game going.

Tommy Byrne

Thirteen years (1943, 46-57)
Born Dec. 31, 1919 BL TL 6'1" 182 lbs.
Position: Pitcher
New York Yankees, St. Louis Browns, Chicago White Sox,
Washington Senators

G	W	L	PCT	ERA	GS	CG	SV	IP	H	BB	SO	BA	FA
281	85	69	.552	4.11	170	65	12	1362	1138	1037	766	.238	.943

*B*yrne won 15 or more games three times with the Yankees. He had 12 career shutouts. In 1955 he led the league with a .762 winning percentage, going 16-5. He led the league in walks in 1949, '50, and '51. He led the league in hit batsmen five times. In 1942, he went 17-4 for Newark of the International League, in spite of leading the league in walks. In 1954, he went 20-10 for Seattle of the Pacific Coast League and led the league in strikeouts. He finished the year with the Yankees, where he completed four of his five starts, going 3-2 with a 2.70 ERA. One of baseball's top-hitting pitchers, he batted .263 as a pitcher. A 6 for 80 mark as a pinch hitter lowered his career batting average to .238.

He hit 14 career home runs, eight triples, and 26 doubles. He pitched in six World Series games, going 1-1 with a 2.53 ERA. He played on four Yankee pennant-winning teams and two World Championship teams.

Flying Insurance

I can remember when the Yankees first started flying, I think in '47. After awhile, the Yankees voted to travel by train. But when we flew, the guys would put money in the machines to get some extra insurance and mail it to their family. Yogi would always put his in his pocket, and he'd applaud when we'd land. He'd say, "There goes another quarter shot to hell." Everybody was really happy to get on the ground.

We had one bad experience on a plane when I was with the Yankees, coming into Chicago. We came in there during a storm, and we were circling around, circling around and it's really raining. Visibility was very bad and the fellas sitting on my side of the plane were looking out into the darkness. It was daytime, but it was just so heavy it looked like darkness. It looked like we missed a big plane. It just went right by us, underneath us, and it looked like it missed us by a hundred feet, but it was probably five or six hundred feet. God, you should have heard everybody yell.

My last three years with the Yankees, I didn't fly, I just stayed on the train. We were still playing from the central part of the country to the East; there were no West Coast teams. I had a houseful of kids and I wanted to one day be able to go home to them. I'd get awful mad if the plane went down.

And I didn't mind riding the train. There was a guy named Jerry Mitchell, a writer for the *New York Post*. He didn't fly. So he and I would ride together, and we'd sit back there in the diner and have a nice dinner, and have a beer or two and talk about this and that. Of course, it took about 20 to 30 hours to get from Kansas City to New York, but we always had an off day in between games.

Tommy Byrne

Bill Veeck

When I was with the Browns, Bill Veeck would be out there at the ballpark and take that leg off, that plastic leg he wore, that fiberglass thing, and he'd put one of those buckets of beer under each arm and you'd see him jumping out in the bleachers from the dugout. Hell, he'd be buying people beer, sitting there chewing the fat. He was a beautiful man. He bought the club and I played there the last half of '51, and I was something like 7 and 11. I worried all winter, trying to figure out how I could keep from taking a cut,— and damn, if he didn't send me a two thousand dollar raise. I couldn't believe it. He was real nice to me.

Later, when I was in the Coast League, I was pitching one night against L.A. in Los Angeles, and I could hear this guy up there near the press box when I was warming up, just before I was going to take a breather and then go out to the mound. I wouldn't look up there, but the guy was really after me, you know, he had a real foghorn voice. I finished warming up and kind of glanced up there, and this guy was waving to me— it was Veeck. He was out there doing some work for Wrigley, I guess. It turned out we beat them 1-0. I hit a home run into centerfield off a knuckleball pitcher. But the point was he came down to the clubhouse, he and the Mrs., and we went out and had dinner after the game. He was something else.

Confrontation

[The highly respected Bill McKinley umpired in the AL from 1946-65.]

The Browns were playing at home against the Red Sox, and I guess it was about the tenth or eleventh inning. I threw a ball right down the middle for strike three, and how in the hell McKinley said "ball" I don't know. I got a bit vocal. He came out to the mound and started mouthing off, and I said, "Well, it's about 94 out here, 95, and I've been working hard all day. Maybe you're getting tired but I'm trying to win the game. How about going back behind home plate?"

The batter swung at the next pitch and popped up, and we got out of the inning.

I came off the mound and I was going right to the dugout. I wasn't going to say anything to McKinley. But he wanted the last word, and he met me at the foul line. He said something to me and without thinking I took my three fingers and just drove them right into that breast protector and I said, "That's where the pitch was."

And I just kept right on walking. If there had been a big crowd there, he might have really popped it to me right there.

Let Them Sleep

Very rarely did any batters charge the mound back then. I just don't understand why hitters are prone to do that. I got hit in the head twice myself. I was just a guy who liked to hit, but they would throw at me because they thought I was throwing at them. Normally, if a hitter got knocked down, he got the impression that you obviously thought something of him. Certain guys, you come close to them, you just wake them up. Sometimes it's better to let them sleep.

Bob Cain

Five years (1949-53)
Born Oct. 16, 1924 BL TL 6'0 165 lbs.
Position: Pitcher
Chicago White Sox, Detroit Tigers, St. Louis Browns

G	W	L	PCT	ERA	GS	CG	SV	IP	H	BB	SO	BA	FA
140	37	44	.457	4.50	89	27	8	628	618	316	249	.196	.975

In 1952 Cain beat Bob Feller 1-0 in a double one-hitter. Bobby Young's first-inning triple was the only Browns hit, and Luke Easter's fifth-inning single was the only Indians hit. In 1950, Bob's first season, he won nine games for the White Sox and ranked third in the American League in fewest hits per nine innings. He won 12 games each of the next two seasons. His 12 wins for the Browns in 1952 tied Satchel Paige for the team lead. In 1951, Bob was involved in one of the strangest at-bats in baseball history. While pitching for the Tigers he walked Eddie Gaedel, a 3'-7" midget signed by Bill Veeck, on four pitches. The following day midgets were banned from baseball.

Eddie Gaedel

It was a complete surprise to the Detroit ballclub when Eddie Gaedel came out to bat. I wasn't paying any attention and neither were any of our other fellas. It was before the second game of a doubleheader and they brought this big cake out in front of the stands and out jumped this little midget. He was wearing a Brownie uniform with the number $1/8$ on it. Well, nobody paid any attention because after he came out of the cake he walked over to the Browns' dugout, and nothing was said.

When we were at bat in the top of the first we noticed something, I did anyway, because they had Frank Saucier playing in the outfield. Well, everybody knew he had a bad arm and couldn't throw, and we thought something was funny. They got us out the top half of the inning, and when the Browns came to bat, they announced that Eddie Gaedel was batting for Frank Saucier. Well, that woke everybody up. We thought it was a big joke.

Ed Hurley, the umpire, got kind of provoked and started over to the Browns' dugout, and Zack Taylor, the manager of the Browns, met him part way and handed him the contract. When Hurley read that contract he just came back and said, "Play Ball."

Bob Swift come out and talked to me, and I asked Bob, "What the heck is it, a joke or what?" I said, "Should I toss underhanded?" He said, "No, this is for real."

Bob went back behind home plate he laid down and put his head on one hand and held his mitt up, and Ed Hurley got on him for doing that and told him he had to get up in his regular stance. Gaedel was standing like Joe DiMaggio, with his feet wide apart, and then Bill Veeck taught him how to squat down. He was only 3'7" to begin with, so there wasn't much of a target there at all.

I walked him on four pitches. I think the first two pitches would have been a strike on an ordinary batter. But the next two I just kind of lobbed in there and we were kind of laughing a little bit, thinking it was such a joke. Then after I walked him he trotted down to first base and he waited until Jim Delsing got down to first to run for him and he patted Delsing on the rear end.

Bob Cain

Their dugout was on the third base side so he had to run across from first base across the infield, and he was tipping his hat to the crowd all the way back. And that woke the crowd up pretty good. Later, Bill Veeck said he told Gaedel that he would be on the roof of the stadium and would shoot him if he swung the bat. After I walked him I gave up another walk and a base hit. I thought I was going to get taken out of that ball game right away. But they didn't score, and we ended up winning the ball game 6-2.

After that everything settled down. The funny part of it is, after the first inning we just went ahead and played a normal ballgame, and nothing was ever said or brought up about it even after that. That was what was so surprising, nobody said anything about it or mentioned anything, but when the commissioner tried to rule that Gaedel was ineligible, and wanted it taken out of the record books, well, that's when Bill Veeck made a big issue out of it, stating that the whole game would be no good then. So Gaedel's at-bat counted, but the next day American League president Will Harridge banned Gaedel "in the best interests of baseball."

Gaedel was murdered up in Chicago ten years later, in 1961. My wife and I were the only two from baseball that went to his funeral. We flew up to his funeral because we felt we had a little obligation to, being connected with him. Bill Veeck would have been there, but he was ill, I think, in Florida. But he did send a big bouquet of flowers there for him.

On July 30, 1994, Mike Veeck, Bill Veeck's son, had my wife and I come up to St. Paul, Minnesota. He was the president of a minor league club there, the St. Paul Saints. He reenacted that same deal his dad pulled. On a Sunday before their game I had my Detroit Tiger uniform and they brought in the manager's son. He was nine or ten years old, about the size of Eddie Gaedel, and had him stand like Eddie Gaedel did and had me pitch four pitches to him. And naturally, I walked him too.

Fish Story

When I pitched with Satchel Paige *[with the Browns in 1952]*, he was a terrific pitcher and a terrific fellow to be around. He could still thread a needle pretty doggone good, and then, of course, he brought up that hesitation pitch, but that came with him getting a little older. But he was still a pretty rough pitcher for a couple innings. And it was strictly because of his uncanny knowledge of the game and his control. He had beautiful control.

Oh, he could still throw a pretty good fast one. It was surprising. I can remember out in spring training one year, Rogers Hornsby was the manager, and he'd holler at old Satch, and Satch would say, "Boss man, I'm going as fast as I can go!" He had his own way of getting in shape and everything. He knew how to get ready, even in exhibition games, especially out in California with the cool and the dampness. Just before he was ready to pitch in a ballgame he'd go in and pour hot water over his wrist, let water run on his wrist for awhile. He'd put some oil on it, what he called his snake oil. He said that's all he needed to warm up. He'd throw maybe one or two pitches and he'd be ready to pitch in the ballgame.

Down there in St. Louis, especially in '53, Bill Veeck told him he didn't have to be at the ballgame until around the fifth inning. Satch liked the idea of going fishing, and this one particular night we were playing a ball game and Satch came in late. After the ballgame we went in to take our shower and the whole shower was filled with fish. Satch had been fishing all day and brought his fish right out to the ballpark and put them in the shower. He was forever pulling stunts such as that.

Andy Carey

Eleven years (1952-62)
Born Oct. 18, 1931   BR   TR   6'1 $\frac{1}{2}$" 190 lbs.
Position: Third Base
New York Yankees, Kansas City Athletics,
Chicago White Sox, Los Angeles Dodgers

G	BA	AB	H	2B	3B	HR	R	RBI	BB	SO	SB	FA
938	.260	2850	741	119	38	64	371	350	268	389	23	.957

A $60,000 Yankee bonus baby, Carey played in four con-secutive World Series, 1955-58. He hit .302 in 1954. In 1955 he led the American League with 11 triples. He tied a major league record for third basemen with four double plays in a 1955 game. He played third base behind Don Larsen in Larsen's perfect game in the 1956 World Series. Carey was with the Yankees from 1952 until 1960, when he was traded to the Athletics for Bob Cerv.

Casey's Purple Pants

Stengel platooned. I remember going five for five in Boston, coming into Yankee Stadium and never knowing if I was going to play or not. I think Stengel respected me because I was fiery and I got mad, but I don't think he liked me because I didn't play anything but third base. He liked his infielders to play more than one position, and he tried to get me to play shortstop. I was hardheaded though, and I refused. Looking back, I'd probably have been better off in learning how to play shortstop. I did not endear myself to the Old Man by only staying with third base.

He had a habit of wearing—when we'd go into a slump, which for us was losing five or six games in a row—he used to put on his purple pants.

I always used to try to wake him up when he was on the bench. I'd go by and yell real loud, and agitate him a little bit. Occasionally, in the latter years, he would sort of doze off a little bit, but even if he wasn't dozing off, I would yell at him, yell at somebody on the field, shake him up a little bit.

Koufax' Style

Herb Score was awesome before his injury. I wouldn't put him in the same category with Koufax, though. Just a notch under. Koufax is the only man I could ever say this about, that every time he went out there, I expected him to throw a no-hitter. I mean, that's every time he went out there. *[From 1962-65 the National League had nine no-hitters, Four were by Koufax, including his perfect game against the Cubs.]* And remember, he was very wild there for a long time. He didn't do much for a long time; his career was really those last seven years. *[Koufax won 36 games in his first six seasons; he won 129 in his last six seasons.]* In those last few years he was awesome, no one could touch him. He had good control, and a fast ball and curve ball. A great curve ball. He gave you that real slow wind-up; he was not a real fast herky-jerky kind of guy. He'd just give that smooth delivery and he'd just let it go and that ball was on top of you.

Ted's Kindness

I'll never forget his kindness to me as a young rookie. I called over to the Boston clubhouse and asked if he would talk to me about hitting. He took over an hour of his time with me. I went out there real early—we sat in the grandstand—and he talked to me about hitting for an hour.

And I went out and hit a home run that day to beat them.

Yeah, They Reserved You

My salary for my first full year in the major leagues, 1953, was five thousand dollars. I hit .321 and I think I got a three thousand dollar raise. When I hit .302 I had to hold out two weeks to get a four thousand dollar raise. The owners in those days were very dominant, and if you didn't like what they gave you, they would just say, "See you later."

They'd either get rid of you or let you die on the vine. It's just the way baseball was in those days. It's something that had been accepted for many, many years, and not really challenged. There wasn't free agency. You had the reserve clause, and they reserved you, all right.

Gil Coan

Eleven years (1946-56)
Born May 18, 1922 BL TR 6'0 180 lbs.
Position: Outfield
Washington Senators, Baltimore Orioles,
Chicago White Sox, New York Giants

G	BA	AB	H	2B	3B	HR	R	RBI	BB	SO	SB	FA
918	.254	2877	731	98	44	39	384	278	232	384	83	.973

Coan hit .303 in both 1950 and 1951 for Washington, where he played the first eight of his 11 big league seasons. After some incredible minor league seasons, the Chicago Cubs offered the Senators $100,000 for him, but Washington refused the offer. In 1944 he hit .367 with 64 RBIs and a league-leading 13 home runs in just 72 games for Kingsport of the Appalachian League before finishing the season with Chattanooga of the Southern Association, where he hit .335 in 48 games. In 1945 for Chattanooga Coan was named Minor League Player of the Year after leading the Southern Association in hits (201), doubles (40), triples (28—a league record), home runs (16), stolen bases (37), and batting average (.372). His 117 RBIs were three off the league lead. After play-

ing with the Senators in 1946, he returned to Chattanooga in 1947, hitting .340 while leading the league with 17 triples and 42 stolen bases. In 11 games for Washington that year he hit .500 (21 for 42). One of the American League's fastest runners, he stole 23 bases, second to Dillinger's league-leading 28. Before the 1954 season he was traded from Washington to Baltimore for Roy Sievers.

Hot Days

Oh, it was hot in St. Louis and Washington! And Chicago was hot lots of times, in the South Side there, close to those stock yards. You could smell them if the wind was blowing the right direction.

In St. Louis we used to go to the grocery store and get a couple of cabbage heads and peel the leaves off them and put them in a bucket of ice. Before going out on the field every inning you'd get a cabbage leaf and put it under your hat. That keeps you kind of cooled off until you can get back to the dugout.

Fenway Nightmare

Playing left field at Fenway was a nightmare because of that wall. You never knew if a ball was going to bounce off it or just drop straight down when it hit it. And if a ball hit one of those spots on the scoreboard, it could ricochet anywhere. In the left field corner, from right behind third base down the line, it's only about two feet between the foul line and the concrete stands. It's dangerous down in there if you're going for a line drive.

I had to play the hitters different in Fenway. You didn't have near the territory to cover out there. You played short enough that almost every left fielder had a chance to throw a runner out at home on a base hit. Usually the runner from second couldn't score on a sharply hit single to left field. Ted Williams was probably the greatest hitter that ever lived, but he was not a good outfielder. Still, he did a credible job every time we saw him play left field in Fenway.

Timing Feller

After the war, they had a big promotion at Cleveland. They timed Bob Feller before a game, the first actual timing of a pitcher, I reckon, in the major leagues or anywhere else. The Army brought a crude device out there. It was set up along home plate with a wooden frame the size of the strike zone, and they had a light. The ball going through the frame broke the beam of light that went from the front of the strike zone to the back; that's were they timed it.

The most amazing thing was, he warmed up out there and then he threw six pitches, and the first five went through for strikes and averaged somewhere between 97 and 98 miles an hour, and the sixth one hit that device and blew it to smithereens.

Jerry Coleman

Nine years (1949-57)
Born Sept. 14, 1924   BR TR 6'0" 165 lbs.
Positions: 2B, 572; SS, 116; 3B, 41
New York Yankees

G	BA	AB	H	2B	3B	HR	R	RBI	BB	SO	SB	FA
723	.263	2119	558	77	18	16	267	217	235	218	22	.973

An All-Star in his second season with the Yankees, Coleman led AL second basemen in fielding his rookie year. He played in 26 World Series games in six World Series with the Yankees, hitting .275 with only one error in 96 chances. Military service cost him three full seasons in World War II and almost two full seasons in 1952-53. After his career he worked in the Yankee front office for three years and was a Yankee broadcaster for nine years. A longtime broadcaster for the San Diego Padres, he took a one-year sabbatical to manage the team in the 1980 season.

Haves and Have Nots

One of the things people don't realize is that there were two leagues in the American League, the haves and the have-nots. The haves were New York and Cleveland and Detroit and Boston, and the have-nots were Washington, St. Louis Browns, Philadelphia Athletics, and the Chicago White Sox, before they became the go-go Sox.

The Yankees feasted on the have-nots. We'd play them 22 times and we'd beat them 18, 19 times. So consequently, the balance in the league was very, very poor. The payroll was so low, though, those clubs could still make money and survive.

That was the one thing, the imbalance in the American League was incredible in those days. The Yankees dominated. What'd we win, 14 of 16 from 1949 to 1964? It was just an overabundance of talent; it all ended up in the same place. I mean, I'm delighted I was in it, but it's not healthy, really. It's better to have more of a balanced league, like you have today.

The Cathedral

I loved to play in Yankee Stadium, except it was 461 feet to center field. If you're Joe DiMaggio or Mickey Mantle you'd probably have a heart attack every time you think about it. I used to watch Mantle and DiMaggio hit balls out there a mile and a half and they're caught easily.

It was like a cathedral, the height of the stands. Of course, there were 30,000 obstructed seats there as well because of the beams that held the upper decks, and they've eliminated those now. When you put 70,000 people in a stadium—and we've had as many as 72 before the fire people got there—it was quite a sight.

I thought Yankee Stadium was the greatest cathedral in the history of sports. It was absolutely majestic. We'd scare the daylights out of most teams that came in there, just from that alone.

Yogi Knew His Business

Yogi was not the character many people say he is. He was a very smart baseball man. Yogi knew his business. He was a very bright man about baseball. He still is.

A lot of guys who are probably intellectually superior have never mastered their profession. So who's smarter, the guy who knows what he's doing in his profession or the guy who thinks he knows what he's doing?

Chuck Diering

Nine years (1947-52, 54-56)
Born Feb. 3, 1923 BR TR 5'10" 165 lbs.
Positions: Outfield, 631; 3B, 36; SS, 12
St. Louis Cardinals, New York Giants, Baltimore Orioles

G	BA	AB	H	2B	3B	HR	R	RBI	BB	SO	SB	FA
752	.249	1648	411	76	14	14	217	141	237	250	16	.984

After batting .305 and leading the Georgia-Florida league with 102 runs scored in 1942, Diering spent the next three years in the military. He played for the Cardinals his first five years in the big leagues, then was traded in December 1951 with Max Lanier to the Giants for Eddie Stanky, who was named the Cardinals' manager. In 1953 he batted .322 in 152 games for Minneapolis of the American Association. He was voted the Baltimore Orioles' Most Valuable Player in 1954. He was one of baseball's best defensive outfielders. In 1955-56 he played 36 games at third base for Baltimore, making only two errors (both in the same inning).

The Almost-Raise

In 1956 when I was with Baltimore, I told Paul Richards, "Paul, I want a raise in my contract." He says, "For your ability now, Chuck, you're at your limit, about what you're worth." I said, "Yeah, Paul, but I'm well-liked and I do have people that come in to watch me play, and I am good for the club." He said, "You're correct, but I can't give you a raise." I said, "Well, I'd like to have a thousand dollar raise." He said, "Okay, I'll send you a contract." He sent me the contract, but it was the same one. I sent it back. And spring training was going to start. I got a telephone call from Paul. He said, "Chuck, you better get your ass down here if you want to play baseball." I said, "What about my contract?" He said, "You're not going to get a raise." So I flew down there, and he sat down and said, "I'll tell you what I'll do. If we draw 500,000 people, I'll give you a thousand dollars." That was the year he sent me back to the minors, so I wasn't there to get the money even if they did draw 500,000.

Learning the Ballparks

I prided myself on my defense, enjoyed being in charge in the outfield. I loved the challenge of learning the grass, of playing the ricochets off the short wall in right at Ebbets Field (a crazy, broken-up park) and off the corrugated sheets of metal at the top of the fence at Shibe Park; of playing the ball that dropped straight down off the screen in front of the pavilion in right center at Sportsman's Park.

Forbes Park was big, about 450 to center. You had to make sure the ball didn't get past you for a sure triple, maybe even a home run. Another park with all kinds of room in center was Baltimore, where I made one of my greatest catches. Mantle hit one that kept

Chuck Diering

going well over 400 feet, and I caught it in the bushes in right center. Later, manager Paul Richards said of how far away from the plate I was when I caught the ball: "They had to send a taxi cab to get him."

At Wrigley the winds and ivy made it a tough outfield. So did the grass, always in bad shape from playing football there. Comisky was a tough center field; the park was built on a dump, and center field was built low, so low that sometimes I could see only the top half of the hitter, like playing uphill. Sometimes fog would set in and I couldn't see the hitter at all. The terrace at Crosley Field was a challenge. One day I forgot about it when I went back for a fly ball. My spikes caught on the incline and I fell on my back. My legs flew up in the air, and while I was sprawled on my back the ball came down between my legs. I made the catch.

Detroit's sprinkler system kept it mostly wet, muddy. Pittsburgh was big—450 to center; you couldn't let the ball get past you because it was a sure triple, even a home run, until they brought the fences in (Kiner's Corner). Yankee Stadium had the best grass of any field; in Sportsman's Park it was hard to grow grass because of the heat.

Defense was different then. Players had to learn when and how to leap into unpadded concrete walls. Natural grass cut down on ground rule doubles, made for more plays at the plate with runners trying to score from first on a double. Bad hops, unpredictable caroms, non-symmetrical fields all made for some interesting baserunning situations; they created more excitement for the fans, back when defense was more of an art.

Joe Dobson

Fourteen years (1939-43, 46-54)
Born Jan. 20, 1917 BR TR 6'2" 197 lbs.
Position: Pitcher
Cleveland Indians, Boston Red Sox, Chicago White Sox

G	W	L	PCT	ERA	GS	CG	SV	IP	H	BB	SO	BA	FA
414	137	103	.571	3.62	273	112	18	2170	2048	851	992	.152	.977

*D*obson was an All-Star in 1948, when he went 16-10 with five of his career 22 shutouts. He won 11 or more games eight times. His best season was 1947, when he went 18-8 with a 2.95 ERA. In the 1946 World Series he went 1-0 in three games, did not allow an earned run in 12 and $^2/_3$ innings, struck out 10, walked just three and allowed only four hits. In 1940 he went to Boston in a trade that sent Jim Bagby to Cleveland. In 1950 he was traded to the White Sox with Dick Littlefield and Al Zarilla for Ray Scarborough and Bill Wight. In 1952 he went 14-10 for the White Sox with a 2.51 ERA and three shutouts.

Oh, Marilyn!

[by Mrs. Joe Dobson]

The whole team had their pictures taken with Marilyn Monroe, and she sent each player a picture of her with him, and on all the other guys she said, "I hope we can do it again."

Well, on Joe's she said, "Let's do it again." Well, Joe loved to Lord and Master over all the guys about that.

'46 World Series

I pitched a complete game in Game 5 of the '46 World Series, giving us a 3-2 lead over the Cardinals. I fooled them all along with curves, a fast one, a change-of-pace ball and a slider and the old atom ball. After that game I guess I was about yea-high off the ground. Because I was just—I was elated with everything. I never was so happy in all my life. It was a big disappointment, though, not to win the Series.

Helping Ted Hit .406

Back in 1941 when I was learning to throw a curve ball, I worked out with Ted every day. Ted would hit against that curve and we'd argue whether pitches were balls or strikes or whether his hits would go for singles or doubles. I like to believe that helped Ted hit .406 that year.

Bobby Doerr

Fourteen years (1937-44, 46-51)
Born Apr. 7, 1918   BR   TR   5'11"   175 lbs.
Position: Second Base
Boston Red Sox

G	BA	AB	H	2B	3B	HR	R	RBI	BB	SO	SB	FA
1865	.288	7093	2042	381	89	223	1094	1247	809	608	54	.980

A nine-time All-Star, Doerr was elected to the Hall of Fame
in 1986. He was one of baseball's finest defensive second
basemen. In his 13 full seasons with the Red Sox, he never batted under
.270, and he hit at least 21 doubles each season. He hit 12 or more
home runs each of his last 12 seasons, twice hitting highs of 27. Six
times he drove in more than 100 runs, with a career-high 120 in 1950.
His career total of 1247 RBIs is 79th on the all-time list. Doerr hit over
.300 three times, with a high of .325 in 1944, when he led the league
with a .528 slugging percentage. He had a league-leading 11 triples in
1950. A durable player, he averaged 142 games a year over a 12-year
stretch. He played four years of minor league ball before joining the Red
Sox in 1937. In his only World Series, the loss to the Cardinals in
1946, he batted .409 in 22 at-bats, with a double and home run.

Pictures on Your Bedroom Wall

In 1937 I joined the Red Sox in Sarasota, Florida, and I remember walking out on the field as an 18-year-old kid at that time and seeing Jimmy Foxx, who you're going to play with, and Joe Cronin and Lefty Grove, the Ferrell brothers, and Higgins, and all those great ballplayers. These are guys that you had their pictures on the wall of your bedroom as a little kid and all of a sudden here you are going to play with them. That was a great thrill.

And then, one of the things that stands in my mind is going into Yankee Stadium for the first time that year, and seeing the stadium. How tremendous it was. You know, out on the Coast where I grew up you never saw ballparks anything like that. Well, you never saw major league baseball. I had played against Joe DiMaggio in the Coast League in '35. But to see that great Yankee team, and to see and play against Lou Gehrig, that was a great thrill.

Losing the Series

Losing the World Series that last game in St. Louis in 1946 and not getting to be on a winning World Series team was a tremendous letdown. We had a good ballclub, but I think that what hurt us was we cinched the pennant early and had about three weeks before the World Series. It's hard to get yourself back into a groove. *[The Red Sox won 104 games and finished 12 games ahead of second-place Detroit.]*

The Cardinals and the Dodgers played in a playoff, a two-out-of-three-game playoff, and the Cardinals were all keyed up and hot going into that series. I think that we had a letdown that we probably didn't realize. I think that hurt us a little bit.

I don't have many regrets about my career, when you think of going in the Hall of Fame, having your number retired, playing in

All-Star games, playing in at least one World Series. The only thing, I thought '48, '49, '50 we had great teams. Just one more pitcher would have made the difference. We'd probably win at least two more pennants, and then surely could have won a World Series.

Team Togetherness

I really enjoyed the train trips. It think it was a great thing for team togetherness. You were like a big family. There would be a certain group playing cards, another group standing back in the corner talking baseball. There would be a few guys that would read. I enjoyed it, and I think the guys back in those days did. Some long trips, Boston to St. Louis, were a little tough, but you had your berth where you could go lay down if you wanted to.

And it was interesting to sit and look at the countryside. It's like the difference of going on the freeway now or going back on the old country roads and seeing the country. Going by planes you don't see much, and by train you used to see quite a bit.

Jim Dyck

Six years (1951-56)
Born Feb. 3, 1922 BR TR 6'2" 200 lbs.
Positions: Outfield, 157; 3B, 147; 1B, 1
St. Louis Browns, Cleveland Indians,
Baltimore Orioles, Cincinnati Reds

G	BA	AB	H	2B	3B	HR	R	RBI	BB	SO	SB	FA
330	.246.	983	242	52	5	26	139	140	131	140	4	.961

*D*yck was named to The Sporting News *Major League All-Rookie team in 1952 at the age of 30, when he hit .269 with 15 home runs as a third baseman-outfielder with the Browns. His career was interrupted for three years for military service. Still, in the minor leagues he was an All-Star at every level in the Yankee organization: D, C, B, A, AA and in three different AAA leagues. He helped preserve Bobo Holloman's 1953 no-hitter (in Holloman's first big league start) with a leaping catch against the left-field wall. Dyck led the Western Association in 1946 with RBIs (104) and batting (.364). In 1951 he led the Texas League in RBIs with 127. In 1955 he hit .378 in 78 games for Indianapolis in the American Association, and hit .279 in 61 games for the Baltimore Orioles.*

Satch, the Fisherman

Bill Veeck loved Satch. Hornsby and Satchel would get in a shouting match. Hornsby would fine him.

Hornsby would say, "That's going to cost you two hundred."

Satch would say, "Make it three."

And Hornsby would say, "That's three."

Satch knew that Veeck was going to give him every penny back. Satch was just like he's pictured in everything you've ever read or saw about him. Just amblin' along, easygoing, and then he could just throw bullets. Even at that age. We figured he was somewhere around 56 in 1952, and no one ever knew.

And he loved to fish. He kept bringing these stories back to the clubhouse about these big catfish he was catching in the Missouri River, and we kept telling him he was pulling our leg. We had a doubleheader scheduled one Sunday, and it was about a hundred degrees by the time the first game started, and when we came to the clubhouse, Satch had brought a 56-pound catfish with him. *[A record was set in 1959 for freshwater catfish, 97 pounds.]* He had it laying in the shower room. I think the doubleheader took almost eight hours, with the break between games.

When we finally got to the shower room after that hot day, boy, it just stunk to high heaven. So we told Satch he didn't have to bring us any more evidence. We'd believe him from then on.

Meeting Rogers Hornsby

Rogers Hornsby was the manager when I joined the Browns my rookie year, 1952. He was all business, there's no question about that, but he just didn't know how to handle men, and he would insult you in front of anybody. The veterans on the ballclub went to Veeck with an ultimatum, and they wouldn't let any of the rook-

Jim Dyck

ies take part. So even though I felt the same way they did, I had no part in it. But they said, "Either get rid of Hornsby or there's going to be some real problems." And Veeck did, Veeck canned him. Hornsby was just ill-mannered and gruff.

I first met Hornsby during spring training that year. I was playing ball in South America when the Browns started camp, I had gotten permission to report late that year, because I was involved in the Caribbean World Series. My mom and dad sent me a copy of the *St. Louis Post Dispatch,* and the headlines said HORNSBY AWAITS DYCK WITH OPEN ARMS, and I thought, "Boy, I'm glad to hear he's anxious to have me on the ballclub."

I reported to Burbank about nine thirty at night. I'd just gotten in off the plane and went to the hotel. I'd never seen him in person, but I recognized him. He was sitting in the lobby in a big overstuffed chair, watching the front door. I came in and went immediately to the desk and was checking in, and I was debating about whether I should just go to bed or should I go over and let him know I was there. I finally decided I'd better go over and let him know.

He had a *Sporting News* in his lap and I walked over and stood in front of him and said, "Mr. Hornsby, I'm Jim Dyck." And I stuck my hand out.

He just looked up at he and said, "Yeah, yeah, I know who in the hell you are. Get your ass to bed. I'll see you on the field in the morning and don't be late." He never shook my hand or anything. I turned around and walked away. That was Rogers.

[Hornsby, a Hall of Fame player, hit a career .358, second place all-time behind Cobb, with 301 home runs. He managed for 14 years, winning 701 and losing 812. In his last eight years as manager, his teams never finished higher than sixth place.]

Here's an example of how Hornsby dealt with people. We broke camp in spring training, and we were heading back to St. Louis. We traveled by train, and we had several exhibition games with the Cubs scheduled along the way. We played an exhibition game in a little town in Texas. I was on third with two outs in the ninth and Hornsby was in the dugout. The batter hit a long fly ball. When he catches it, the game's over. So when I crossed the plate the guy caught the ball, and I went kept going right to the bus. Hornsby somehow had beaten me from the dugout through the gate to the bus, and there was an old man, at least in his seventies, standing there, with a scrapbook that must have been five or six inches thick.

He stopped Hornsby at the door to the bus and said, "Mr. Hornsby, would you sign this book for me? You've been my idol all my life, and I've got everything I could ever get out of the papers and magazines about you, and I'd sure like to have your personal autograph on this book."

Hornsby gave him a shove and said, "Get the f--- out of my way!" and through the door he went. I was right behind him and I caught the whole thing. He was just that kind of guy.

How to Break a Losing Streak

In 1953, when I was with the Browns we had a long losing streak, and we were playing the Yankees, who had won 18 straight. Milt Richmond, who was later inducted into the Hall of Fame of sportswriters, was covering our games. He was a good friend of Marty Marion, and he asked Marty who was going to play today, so he could write the story.

Marty said, "It don't make any difference how I make out the lineup, we'd just lose. Why don't you make out the lineup?"

So Milt made out the lineup, and that's when we broke the streak.

A Phone Call to Ford Frick

I was with the Browns in 1953, but in April of '54 I was traded to Cleveland and spent that season in the International League at Richmond, Virginia. The way I got over there was kind of weird. Bob Kennedy was an outfielder, and he played some infield too, with Cleveland. They had a player they wanted to bring up, and they had to let a veteran go. Bob had been with Cleveland for a long time, and they didn't want to get him out of the big leagues, so they made a deal with Baltimore and got me. I was 32 at the time. Baltimore agreed to keep Kennedy in the big leagues and Cleveland didn't hesitate to send me to the International League immediately. So the reason the trade was made wasn't because Cleveland wanted me; it was because they wanted to keep Kennedy in the big leagues. I had a good season at Richmond, and Cleveland brought me back down the stretch drive, and I got to pinch hit one time and I got a base hit, but I was ineligible for the World Series. That was my experience with Cleveland.

The next spring they didn't even take me to camp; they just said, "You can go to Indianapolis." Triple A. I was making pretty good money at the time in Triple A. I got over there, and boy, they couldn't get me out. I was hitting the ball all over the place *[Dyck hit .378 with 17 home runs in 78 games for Indianapolis]*.

So I get a call from Cleveland in late June, early July, and they say, "Meet us in Kansas City." I fly to Kansas City. I walk in a hotel and Feller's standing there. He says, "Come here, Jim, I've got something to tell you that's bad news."

I say, "What's the problem?"

He says, "Well, we can't take you."

I say, "What do you mean? They sent for me."

He says, "Well, there's a rule that if you've been optioned out by the major league club and your options have been all used up, then they can't recall you until you go through the winter league draft. But that rule was devised to keep a player in the big leagues, not keep him out." So Feller says, "Let's go up to my room, and we'll call the commissioner in New York, Ford Frick."

We called the commissioner.

Bob says, "You talk to him, but you repeat what he says so I can advise you what to say back to him."

The commissioner says, "Well, you're right, the rule is made to keep players in the big leagues, and it's keeping you out. But I just don't have the authority to change the rule."

I say, "You don't have the authority to change the rule?"

Feller says to me, "Tell him he ain't got a gut in his body if he don't."

I say, "Well, I'm sorry, Commissioner, but if you don't change that rule then you haven't got a gut in your body."

He paused for a minute, and then he says, "You know what? You're right. I can't change the rule, but I can do something to get you in the big leagues. I can make them sell you to another club."

They sold me to Baltimore, so I wound back at Baltimore again. *[Most of Dyck's big league career had been with St. Louis, who moved to Baltimore in 1954. Dyck was sold to Baltimore on July 6, 1955.]*

Del Ennis

Fourteen years (1946-59)
Born June 8, 1925 BR TR 6'0 195 lbs.
Position: Outfield
Philadelphia Phillies, St. Louis Cardinals,
Cincinnati Reds, Chicago White Sox

G	BA	AB	H	2B	3B	HR	R	RBI	BB	SO	SB	FA
1903	.284	7254	2063	358	69	288	985	1284	597	719	45	.969

A three-time All-Star, In 1946 Ennis hit .313 with 17 home runs and won the TSN Rookie Award in the first year it was given. He drove in more than 100 runs nine times. During the 1950s only four players (Snider, Hodges, Berra, Musial) had more RBI. He also hit 20 or more home runs nine times in his career. In the Phillies' pennant-winning season of 1950, Ennis hit .311 with 31 home runs and a league-leading 126 RBIs. He twice had 10 or more triples in a single season. In his first 12 seasons, he never hit fewer than 20 doubles. He had 10 or more outfield assists nine times. In his only minor league season, 1943, he hit .346 with 18 home runs and 16 triples for Trenton, then spent two years in the Navy. In 1956 he was traded to the Cardinals for Bobby Morgan and Rip Repulski. In 1958 he was involved in a trade with the Reds that sent George Crowe, Alex Kellner, and Alex Grammas to the Cardinals.

Eating in the Outfield

The fans used to throw me sandwiches out in left field—they used to throw food out all the time, from the bleachers. They'd throw sandwiches out and I would agitate them by picking them up and eating a couple of them.

Redemption

The great thing about baseball is that you play every day, and you come up to bat four or five times a game. So there are plenty of chances to redeem yourself if you make a mistake.

Once in 1950 against St. Louis, I dropped a fly ball with the bases loaded in the ninth inning, and I came up in the bottom of the ninth with two on against Gerry Staley. I just knew I was going to hit a home run to make up for the error.

And I hit one. *[That was one of the career-high 31 home runs Ennis hit that season. He led the league with 126 RBIs.]*

The Fall

For a moment I thought I had gone from my best day in baseball to my worst day in life itself in a matter of minutes that July day *[July 23]* in 1955 when I hit three home runs in one game and drove in all seven runs in our 7-3 win.

I had taken Del Jr., a little tough feisty kid, to the ballpark with me for the first time. Still on the field after the game ended, still thrilling to the accomplishments of a great game, and the vic-

Del Ennis

tory, I heard over the PA system the announcement that someone had fallen out of the stands from the second deck. I knew it was Del, Jr. I just *knew* it was, and I went from elation to the greatest fear I had ever known.

I was lucky to find out it wasn't him, but I always hoped that the person who had fallen was okay.

There are plenty of things more important than the results of a baseball game.

Beans' Lesson

One day at Ebbets Field, Beans Reardon was behind the plate. The first pitch was high up over my head. He called it a strike. The second pitch, same place. Strike two. I said, "Beans, what—"

He said, "Oh, don't worry about it, kid. You got one more."

I swung at the next pitch and missed.

I turned toward him, but before I could say anything, he said, "I told you you had three."

Don Ferrarese

Eight years (1955-62)
Born June 19, 1929   BR   TL   5'9"   170 lbs.
Position: Pitcher
Baltimore Orioles, Cleveland Indians, Chicago White Sox,
Philadelphia Phillies, St. Louis Cardinals

G	W	L	PCT	ERA	GS	CG	SV	IP	H	BB	SO	BA	FA
183	19	36	.345	4.00	50	12	5	506.2	449	295	350	.156	.952

With a great fastball and one of baseball's best curveballs, Ferrarese was hampered early in his career by control problems and later by arm trouble. He walked 567 batters in his first 522 professional innings, while striking out 502. He walked just five per nine innings in the major leagues. In 1954 he won 18 games and batted .300 for Oakland in the Pacific Coast League. In 1955 for San Antonio in the Texas League he walked 47 in 99 innings, going 9-0 with a 1.48 ERA. In his big league start he struck out 13 men, but lost to Cleveland 2-1. On the same day that Carl Erskine pitched a no-hitter against the Giants in 1956, Don lost a no-hitter against the Yankees in the ninth inning on an infield hit by Andy Carey but won the game 1-0 on Don's RBI off Turley. In a 1959 game he hit three consecutive doubles off Dick Donovan.

Andy Carey, Spoiler

My first major league start was against Cleveland. I struck out 13 and lost 2-1. Four days later I'm in Yankee Stadium, warming up, and Casey Stengel, the manager of the Yankees, came by and patted me on the butt, because he's the guy that signed me, in '48. I start the ninth inning with a no-hitter. We were leading 1-0. I drove the only run in off Turley. The first hitter up is Andy Carey, who went to college with me at St. Mary's College in Maragua. I had him two strikes and I threw him a good curve ball, and it hit the rubber on the plate, bounced in fair territory so high that by the time I caught the ball, looking into the sun, he crossed first base with the first hit.

Billy Martin came up, and he said, "Hey, Casey, hell, I hit Ferrarese in high school, I can hit that guy." I struck his butt out. We had to laugh about that later, because I became his roommate in Cleveland. Don Larsen, who played with me in Hawaii and hit a couple home runs off me in Hawaii said, "Case, let me hit that guy, I can hit him." And he popped up. Then Hank Bauer came up. And he got a single over third base. He broke his bat. So here I am, first and second. I had just lost the game before 2-1. And here comes Mickey Mantle. I said, "Oh, my God." Anyhow, I got him out, a fly ball, and won the game 1-0. It was quite a thrill. That was my first major league win.

Another thing to that story. Carl Erskine of the Dodgers was pitching a no-hitter against the Giants in the Polo Grounds, and we were simultaneously on national television. People were going back and forth, watching these double no-hitters. In the ninth inning, Hank Thompson, the third baseman for the Giants, hit a home run and at the last second went foul, just by the skin of his hair, and Carl got the no-hitter. We would have made a bundle of money. In fact, they'd still be talking about it, trivia, being the double no-hitters. *[On June 29, 1990, Dave Stewart of Oakland pitched a 5-0 no-hitter against Toronto. Later that same day, Fernando Valenzuela of the Dodgers no-hit the Cardinals 6-0.]* That would have been the first time that two no-hitters would have been pitched in the same town.

Mantle's Speed and Power

Mantle's the best I ever saw. Once I saw him hit a single through the box in the 12th inning, just a routine single, and we looked up and he was standing on second base. It was not human and he did it. Even with his bad legs. If he was healthy, he could have stolen every base.

He hit a home run off me three and two in Yankee Stadium in 1956, the year he won the Triple Crown, and they wrote a book about Mickey, all the five hundred and whatever home runs he hit, and the man that wrote the book wrote me, because he saw me in the box score, and I said, "Yeah, there was a special time in Yankee Stadium, and he hit right handed against me, and I threw him a change, three and two, I fooled him totally, and with one hand he hit the ball 415 feet. And everybody just went, "My God, how can a man do that?"

Who, Me?

[Frank Dascoli, a respected National League umpire for 15 years, had the distinction of kicking out basketball star Bill Sharman, who had been called up by the Dodgers. Sharman left with the other Dodgers when Dascoli cleared the bench. Thus Sharman is the only player to ever be ejected from a big league game without ever appearing in one.]

I was the starting pitcher in Philadelphia against the Pirates. I got into the seventh or eighth inning. Dascoli kept calling balls that I thought were strikes. I'd look at him sort of funny, because I didn't want to make him mad at me. I did just enough not to get kicked out.

The next night he was the third base umpire. I'm in the bullpen with Robin Roberts and we're out there talking. I'd pitched my seven, eight innings the day before, so I knew I wasn't going to pitch that night. I'm out there relaxing with my shoes untied, and I see a disturbance. Dascoli's looking over to our dugout, and he goes over there and says, "Ferrarese's out of there!"

Nobody moved.

Mauch says, "Ferrarese's in the bullpen."

Dascoli says, "I don't care where he is, he's out of the game anyhow." So now they're waving to the bullpen for me, and I couldn't hear what they wanted, so I say, "Geez, I can't pitch, I just pitched yesterday."

Here I was in the bullpen, and I got kicked out of the game. I had to leave. I found out it was Chris Short that was agitating him, and Dascoli thought it was me, trying to get even with him for the night before.

Tom Ferrick

Nine years (1941-42, 46-52)

Born Jan. 6, 1915   BR   TR   6'2 1/2"   220 lbs.

Position: Pitcher

Philadelphia Athletics, Cleveland Indians, St. Louis Browns,
Washington Senators, New York Yankees

G	W	L	PCT	ERA	GS	CG	SV	IP	H	BB	SO	BA	FA
323	40	40	.500	3.47	7	4	56	674	654	227	245	.184	.953

*F*errick signed in 1936 and was 26 years old when he joined Connie Mack's Athletics in 1941. He started four games among his 36 appearances and pitched one shutout, winning eight and losing 10. He started only three more games during the next eight seasons. He spent three years in the Navy and returned to go 4-1 in 1946. He came to the Yankees on June 15, 1950 in an eight-player trade with the Browns and played a key role in their pennant and World Series wins. He went 8-4 in relief with nine saves in 30 relief appearances during the rest of the season. He won Game 3 of the World Series in relief of Lopat. On June 15, 1951 he went to Washington with Fred Sanford and Bob Porterfield for Bob Kuzava. Ferrick was a pitching coach in the big leagues for twelve years and then became a longtime scout.

Keeping Afloat

I was lucky to get to pitch for the Yankees in 1950 on that World Championship team. I was up in years pretty much, I was about 36 or 37 at that time. I was with second division teams most of my life. I was with the Browns in 1950 and in midyear the Yankees made a deal for me. I don't know whether it was worth it or not because they gave four players for the two of us, and $50,000. *[Actually, Ferrick, Joe Ostrowski, Leo Thomas, Sid Schacht went to the Yankees, though only Ferrick and Ostrowski stayed with the Yankees that year; while Jim Delsing, Don Johnson, Duane Pillette, and Snuffy Stirnweiss went to the Browns].*

Well, the Browns needed money more than they needed players, to keep them afloat. That was part of it. But the strange thing that happened, was when they made the deal, they made it in St. Louis, and all I did was change clubhouses. That very night I was in the ballgame with the Yankees after being with the Browns up until midday when the deal was made. I went in that night and relieved Vic Raschi in a game and saved the ballgame for them. Things happened pretty quickly.

Marvin Miller

I made $3,000 my first year, in 1941, and you can look at some of the salaries of DiMaggio and those guys—they weren't making a lot of money. Because naturally the income wasn't there, from the revenue from TV and radio, until 1950. In 1946 a lot of us got together on each club and we started the major league pension plan. The premiums were very little. We would get paid our premiums according on the number of years we had in the league and the owners matched that. So when it came to 1950 with the first World Series television and radio contract, the players had a meeting with Happy Chandler. He went to the owners and said that the players would like to have some of that money from the World Series pot to put it into the pension plan. That's what got it afloat. At that time, the benefit was $100 a month for 10 years in the big leagues. And that wasn't much. So as we went along, we raised it to two-fifty for ten years. But it took $13 million to pay that back service, and the players in those days generously donated their service to two All-Star games. And the revenue from that went into the pension plan. It kept it afloat and it kept building it. But then down the road the current day players cut the older players off that thing. So that was the beginning of the greedy situation. And they brought in Marvin Miller. And that was another downfall.

A little story connected with that—Birdie Tebbetts was a smart, smart man, managing the Cleveland baseball club. And Miller was going around to see if the players would accept him as their representative. Birdie said, "Marvin Miller contacted me. He said he'd like to have a meeting with the players." Birdie asked him when he wanted it. He named a time and Birdie said, "I can't do it then because I'm in a workout. I'm not going to stop having a workout and have Marvin Miller take over." They did have the meeting in the clubhouse. Birdie was present, and the coaches and the players. Marvin Miller said to Birdie, "You know, you're the manager, you shouldn't be here." Birdie said, "Let me ask you something, Marvin. Is this going to revolve around the pension plan, too?" He said, "Yes." So Birdie left. But the coaches stayed and got the information. Then after Marvin left, Birdie had a meeting with all his players on the Cleveland club. He talked to them about what would happen if he brought a labor man in. He said, "You're going to have strike after strike after strike." And he predicted right. After Marvin left they voted and they were one of the few clubs that didn't vote to bring Marvin Miller in.

Bonus from Mr. Mack

I played for Connie Mack my first year in the big leagues. Connie sat on the bench in his civilian clothes, very calm and sedate, and he knew what was going on at all times. I liked him as a manager and as a person. In fact, in 1941 I had a reasonable year with a last-place club. I was eight and 10 and I saved some ballgames for them *[seven saves]*, pretty good on that ballclub. Near the end of the year they put me on waivers, and they never called me off them. The Cleveland club claimed me for $7,500. So the last two weeks of the season I had to go out to join the Cleveland club, and they wanted to make sure my arm was sound, so all I did was pitch batting practice and never got in a game.

So I came back to Philadelphia to live because I was single. I was working at a plant that made submarine batteries before I enlisted in the Navy. And one day during the winter Mr. Mack's secretary called me. I went down to Mr. Mack's office in Shibe Park. I went up to his office in the tower and sat down and we exchanged pleasantries. Then he said to me, "Tom, I didn't give you any bonus when you signed, so I'm going to give you something now." He gave me a check for a thousand dollars. And he wasn't obligated for it. But he was a great guy to play for, a great human being. It was really a thrill to play for him.

Boo Ferriss

Six years (1945-50)
Born Dec. 5, 1921 BL TR 6'2" 208 lbs.
Position: Pitcher
Boston Red Sox

G	W	L	PCT	ERA	GS	CG	SV	IP	H	BB	SO	BA	FA
144	65	30	.684	3.64	103	67	8	880	914	314	296	.250	.979

*A*n All-Star in 1946, Ferriss won 46 games in his first two seasons in the majors, going 21-10 his rookie season and following it with a 25-6 mark in 1946, with a league-leading winning percentage of .806. In the 1946 World Series he shut out the Cardinals 4-0 in Game Three and had a 2.03 ERA in 13 $^1/_3$ innings in the Series. Arm trouble shortened his big league career, but among pitchers in the 20th century who pitched at least 880 innings, his winning percentage is fourth best all-time, behind only Spud Chandler, Whitey Ford, and Don Gullett. A fine hitting pitcher, he batted .250 for his career and was used by the Red Sox 41 times as a pinch hitter. He set a record for most consecutive wins at one ballpark, 13 in a row at Fenway Park. He was pitching coach with the Red Sox from 1955 to 1959 and was baseball coach at Delta State in Mississippi for 26 years.

Boo Ferriss

Ted Williams' Inside-the-Park Home Run

I was with the Red Sox when we clinched the '46 pennant in Cleveland out in old League Park, the bandbox. Tex Hughson shut out the Indians 1-0 and our lone run was on Ted Williams' inside-the-park home run. Unbelievable. He hit a line drive right over the third baseman's head and they had the Williams shift on and he circled the bases before they could retrieve it. The left fielder was playing way over in center field. That was something to see—those long legs of Ted's trying to make it all the way in. He wasn't the fastest guy running those bases. That might have been his only in-side-the-park home run. Circumstances had to be just right.

Bob Friend

Sixteen years (1951-66)
Born Nov. 24, 1930   BR   TR   6'0"   190 lbs.
Position: Pitcher
Pittsburgh Pirates, New York Yankees, New York Mets

G	W	L	PCT	ERA	GS	CG	SV	IP	H	BB	SO	BA	FA
602	197	230	.461	3.58	497	163	11	3611	3722	894	1734	.121	.969

A three-time All-Star, Bob averaged over 15 wins a season for the Pirates from 1955-64, winning at least 13 in nine of those 10 seasons. One of baseball's most durable pitchers, he pitched at least 200 innings in eleven straight seasons. He pitched 36 shutouts, including a league-leading five in 1962. In 1955 he led the NL with a 2.83 ERA, the first pitcher to ever to accomplish the feat pitching for a last-place team. In 1958 he tied Spahn in wins with 22. In 1960 he helped lead the Pirates to a pennant with 18 wins, including seven in the final two months of the season. He was the winning pitcher in the 1956 and 1960 All-Star games. In the 1956 he recorded his last three outs by striking out three left-handed batters in succession—Mickey Mantle, Yogi Berra, and Ted

ated from Purdue University. The Pirates' player representative, he went on to a successful career in local politics in Pittsburgh after his playing career ended.

'60 World Series

In 1960 we had a great ballclub and won so many games in the late innings. The crowning thing of my whole career was being on that championship team. Hal Smith hit that three-run homer. That was such a big home run because it put us back in the game. *[Smith's home run in the bottom of the eighth inning of the seventh game gave the Pirates a 9-7 lead.]* And they erased it; the Yankees came back and tied it up. It was a Series where they scored a lot of runs. They murdered us in some games and then we ended up winning the Series. *[The Yankees outscored the Pirates 55 to 27 but lost the Series.]* We made some great plays, defensive plays, and got the key hits. We sat in the dugout and watched Maz—we watched that thing go over Yogi Berra's head for a home run. It's the first time a Series had ended with a home run.

Danny Gardella

Three years (1944-45, 50)
Born Feb. 26, 1920 BL TL 5'7 $\frac{1}{2}$" 160 lbs.
Positions: OF, 119; 1B, 15
New York Giants, St. Louis Cardinals

G	BA	AB	H	2B	3B	HR	R	RBI	BB	SO	SB	FA
169	.267	543	145	12	3	24	74	85	57	68	2	.957

In his second season, 1945, Gardella hit .272 for the Giants in 121 games and hit 18 home runs. A complex, religious and philosophical man of artistic temperament, he refused the Giants' offer of $4,500 in 1946 and jumped to the Mexican League for $10,000. When he was suspended by Commissioner Chandler, he sued baseball, challenging its reserve clause. The Gardella v. Chandler antitrust case was dismissed by a district court in 1948, but baseball settled out of court with Gardella, paying him $29,000 and lifting his suspension. He played for the Cardinals in 1950 but appeared in only one game, batting once as a pinch hitter. His was the only successful challenge to baseball's reserve clause in the federal courts. He said, "I may have sued baseball, but as our Lord says, 'I chastised you because I love you.'"

Cinderella Boy

When I was a player, the kid in me was thrilled to ecstasy when I catapulted into the wonderful, dark, mysterious million-seated Polo Grounds. It was religious to round the bases after a homer. I was a Cinderella boy, Mel Ott was my Prince, and the Polo Grounds my grand palace. Truly, I believe God Himself put me there. I tell you, words will not adequately describe the grand elation of my joy at being in the majors in my hometown, New York.

One of my big thrills came at the Polo Grounds. They had announced that the game was to be called after that inning for darkness, and I hit a last-out home run to win the game. Ernie Lombardi, a kindhearted giant, handed me $20, a sweet gesture, for salaries were terribly cheap!

Ned Garver

Fourteen years (1948-61)
Born Dec. 25, 1925   BR   TR   5'10 $^1/_5$"   180 lbs.
Position: Pitcher
St. Louis Browns, Detroit Tigers, Kansas City Athletics,
Los Angeles Angels

G	W	L	PCT	ERA	GS	CG	SV	IP	H	BB	SO	BA	FA
402	129	157	.451	.373	330	153	12	2477.1	2471	881	881	.218	.961

Garver pitched 18 big league shutouts. He won 20 games for the Browns in 1951, hitting .305. The only 20th century pitcher to win 20 games for a team which lost 100, one of his seven big league home runs helped him win his 20th game. He was on the All-Star team in 1951. His $25,000 contract in 1952 made him the highest-paid Brown in history. He led the American League in complete games in 1950 and 1951. He won 10 or more games eight times, all with second division teams.

The Kindness of Umpires

Late in my career with the Angels we were playing in Minneapolis. They called me in from the bullpen, and I hadn't had time to warm up. Once I got to the mound the umpire was supposed to let me have only about seven more warm-up pitches.

Well, as I got to the mound the umpire waited until I'd thrown several pitches, then he walked clear back to the stands to the ballboy and got some more baseballs. He did it on purpose to give me more time to warm up. That's the kind of thing that meant something, an umpire giving you a break like that.

Life in the Minors

In the lower minors, the lights were poor, the meal money was bad, and it was tough. You didn't think about it at the time. I thought I was having a big time. But by the same token, when I look back on it, I'd hate to do that again. You go out and you'd have 25 cents for breakfast, and 50 cents for lunch, and 75 cents for an evening meal, and have to take care of your own laundry and everything. Sometimes we'd stay in bad hotels. Sometimes a hotel wouldn't take you and we'd stay in a rooming house and the dad-blamed bedbugs would eat you up. Once in Class D, two of us slept in the same bed and it wasn't even a full-sized bed. The only way you could sleep in there is if you turned on your side. If both of you slept on your back, there wouldn't be room enough.

Some of the clubhouse facilities were pretty bad. I can remember some places where we'd have to hang our shoes and our gloves on wires that ran across the clubhouse so that the rats wouldn't eat on them overnight. There were no really good facilities in the minor leagues.

Randy Gumpert

Ten years (1938-38, 46-52)
Born Jan. 23, 1918   BR   TR   6'3" 185 lbs.
Position: Pitcher
Philadelphia Athletics, New York Yankees, Chicago White Sox,
Boston Red Sox, Washington Senators

G	W	L	PCT	ERA	GS	CG	SV	IP	H	BB	SO	BA	FA
261	51	59	.464	4.17	113	47	7	1052.2	1099	346	352	.182	.951

An All-Star in 1951 with the White Sox, Gumpert had his best season with the Yankees in 1946 (11-3 with a 2.31 ERA. In 1949 he completed 18 of his 32 starts with the White Sox and pitched three of his six career shutouts. He pitched 36 games for the Athletics between 1936-38, but did not get back to the major leagues until 1946 (he spent '43, '44 and '45 in military service). Before signing with the Athletics in 1936, he pitched two years of batting practice for the A's in Shibe Park.

Bobo Newsom

Bobo Newsom won a lot of games and he lost a lot of games. He was like Babe Ruth, he didn't know anybody's name. He called everybody Bo. One peculiarity about him I remember, if there was anything around the mound—like if it was a windy day and there was a piece of paper that there—he'd go and pick it up and put it in his pocket. There was a fellow in the league by the name of Roger "Doc" Cramer, who was a cut-up from the word go. *[Cramer played 20 years, had 2705 hits and batted .296.]* He'd always throw all these torn-up pieces of paper on the mound when Newsom was pitching.

Well, Newsom spent more time picking up the paper than he did pitching, really. That was kind of a fetish he had; he had to keep everything in order around the mound. He didn't remember who you were, but he was a good pitcher. *[In Newsom's 20-year big league career he won 211, lost 222, and pitched, in this order, for the following teams: Dodgers, Cubs, Browns, Senators, Red Sox, Browns, Tigers, Senators, Dodgers, Browns, Senators, Athletics, Senators, Yankees, Giants, Senators, Athletics. He was a 20-game winner three times and a 20-game loser three times.]*

Battle of the Youngest

My first year, 1936, was also Bob Feller's first year, and we were playing out in Cleveland. Mr. Mack talked to the Cleveland people and said, "Here are two youngest ballplayers in the league. It might add a few people to the gate if we have them pitch against each other."

Feller was 17 and I was 18, so we pitched against each other and he beat me 5-2. It would have been 3-2 but our shortstop Russ Peters made a wild throw with two men on and two out. Two runs

Randy Gumpert

scored, and that made it 5-2, and it could have been 3-2. It wasn't a bad ballgame.

The next day in Chicago, Mr. Mack was in the lobby of our hotel, and—he called me Rand—he said, "Come on, Rand, we'll go have a bite to eat." So I went in with him and had a bite to eat, and he was talking to me about the game, and he said, "You know, it didn't look to me like you were throwing as hard as you usually do."

I said, "You know, maybe I wasn't, but I felt all right." But I thought to myself, in that particular game Feller struck out 17. So there's a 17-year-old boy striking out 17 big leaguers. I struck out two, and those two were Feller. So no wonder I didn't look like I was throwing as hard if Feller was striking out 17.

Looks Aren't Everything

Berra was with Newark in '46. They didn't know what to do with him; they didn't know if he was a catcher or an outfielder. But finally they decided that catching was his best position, and Bill Dickey worked with him in '47 when he came up to the Yankees.

Yogi was a good catcher. They kind of made him seem like a buffoon, with the sayings that are attributed to him; whether he said them or whether they were made up by the sportswriters, nobody really knows.

But he was a very good ballplayer, and that was all that was expected from him. Like somebody said, "Well, you don't look like a ballplayer," and he said, "Well, you don't hit with your face."

'47 World Series & '51 All-Star Game

I was on the Yankees roster in the 1947 World Series against the Dodgers. It went seven games. I didn't get in any games, but I was there on the ballclub, and I think we got about $5,200, winner's share. So that was a help. Back then you could buy a few things with $5,200.

Then I was named to the 1951 All-Star team. *[Five other White Sox players were named to the All-Star game that year: Nellie Fox, Jim Busby, Minnie Minoso, Eddie Robinson, Chico Carrasquel.]* I had won seven and lost none at that time, so they picked me as one of the pitchers. But I didn't get in that game either.

They were telling me something, I think. *[The AL used five pitchers in an 8-3 loss: Ned Garver, Eddie Lopat, Fred Hutchinson, Mel Parnell, Bob Lemon.]*

Dick Hall

Sixteen years (1955-57, 59-71)
Born Sept. 27, 1930 BR TR 6'6" 200 lbs.
Position: Pitcher (OF, 119; 2B, 7; 3B, 5; 1B, 1)
Pittsburgh Pirates, Kansas City Athletics,
Baltimore Orioles, Philadelphia Phillies

G	W	L	PCT	ERA	GS	CG	SV	IP	H	BB	SO	BA	FA
495	93	75	.554	3.32	74	20	68	1259	1152	236	741	.210	.976

*H*all *pitched for four pennant-winning teams in Balti more and pitched in the 1969, 1970, and 1971 World Series. Signed as an outfielder with Pittsburgh, he played three minor league seasons as an outfielder. In his first year of pitching, he led the Western League with a .706 winning percentage and a 2.24 ERA. In 1959 he led the Pacific Coast League with 18 wins and a 1.87 ERA. In 1963 with the Orioles he went 5-5 with 12 saves and a 2.98 ERA while batting .464 (13-28). In his final 462 major league innings, he unintentionally walked only 23 batters. For his entire career, he averaged only 1.69 walks per nine innings.*

Maris' Bid for 60

In '61 when Maris hit the 61 home runs Bowie Kuhn said, well, he has to do it in 154 games, because that's what Babe Ruth had. Well, the 154th game was here in Baltimore, and he had 58 coming into that game. Pappas started. It was kind of a bad night, kind of rainy, and the wind was blowing in from right, which made it tough, but he hit one off Pappas, number 59. Pappas got knocked out early in the game, so I came in and pitched, and it was the weirdest game, because it was like an exhibition game, except when Maris came up. Then it was like a World Series game. There was so much tension with him trying to break the record, it was really strange. Everybody sort of went through the motions, and oh-oh, here comes Maris up, now—now it's like the bottom of the ninth in the seventh game of the World Series, every time he batted.

We'd argued ahead of time, if he gets up and has a chance to break the record are you going to walk him, are you going to let him hit the ball, or what? Some of the guys said, "I don't want my name in the record book, I'd walk him."

But I figured I'd be fair to him, and I faced him twice. And every single pitch I threw was hittable. I think he struck out, and then he hit a line drive right at the right fielder. He did get to bat once more, against Hoyt Wilhelm. He had a little checked swing and hit a little dribbler back to the mound. So he ended up with 59. In the last eight games he hit two more. They finally got rid of the asterisk.

Whitey Herzog had played with Maris and I had played with Herzog at Kansas City. We'd both been traded to Baltimore. There was so much pressure, media pressure, that the night before that game, he decided he didn't want to stay in the hotel. So he stayed with Herzog. I lived north of town, so I'd pick up Herzog and Russ Snyder on the way to the ballpark every day. So I picked up Herzog this game, and here was Maris. I drove Maris to the ballpark that day. Because of the pressure and everything, little round patches of his hair were starting to fall out.

Weaver's 25-Man Team

The best manager I played for was Earl Weaver. He was the best at using everybody. There's so many games that you really need all 25 guys. You never know when somebody's going to get hurt, or you need a pinch hitter. He would give everybody on the club what is like a starter's role, even if it was a minor one. Like in my case, he had it down to where I only pitched in the seventh inning in close games, or else I'd come in in extra inning games. He had a couple of pitchers, short men, who would pitch the eighth and ninth, and he had long men from the first through the sixth, so I was a seventh inning pitcher.

So if it got to that situation where he needed a pitcher in the seventh inning I was in effect the starter in that situation. The most famous case, I think, was Skaggs. Dave Skaggs. He was the starting catcher when Denny Martinez pitched. Weaver didn't have a computer so much then, but he kept his little notebook, and somehow he came up with that idea that Martinez pitched better when Skaggs was catching. That information was really very useful, because your catcher can't catch every game.

So when Etchebarren was set down for Martinez's start, he wasn't going to get upset because he figures, well, what Weaver says makes sense. He's really the best catcher for that situation. Skaggs is kind of a scrub but he knows that every fifth game he's a starter, so he has his starter's role on the club, in effect.

And Weaver had Curt Motton as a pinch hitter. Motton wasn't much of an outfielder, no power, but he was a pretty good hitter. *[Motton batted .303 in 1969.]* He got a few key hits late in the game, so Weaver said, "Here's my man. If we really need somebody to get on base in the late innings, Motton's my key thing. And he makes Motton believe this, and everybody else believes this. *[Motton hit .213 lifetime, but he went 8-25 as a pinch hitter for the Orioles in 1969.]*

I think it helped us. It was sort of self-fulfilling. I think Weaver was real good in that respect. He used everybody. Everybody had a role. Everybody stayed happy, and everybody stayed ready.

Throwing Strikes

[Of everyone who pitched more than 1,250 innings, Dick Hall's ratio of fewest walks per nine innings is 22nd best in history.]

Mostly I think you're born with good control. When I was a little kid I used to throw a tennis ball against the steps and make believe I was pitching. I think that helped a little bit. When I first started pitching I averaged maybe two walks a game, which is good, and by the end of my career I was averaging about a half a walk a game.

Part of it's concentration, too. You just make up your mind that you're not going to walk them. At the end of my career basically I threw every single pitch on the outside corner, as hard as I could throw it. You always hear, "Get ahead of the hitters," and it's really vitally important. The better the hitter, the more important it is that you get ahead of him. I just said, "I'm not going to walk people, they get enough hits as it is without getting people on base."

Gail Harris

Six years (1955-60)
Born Oct. 15, 1931   BL   TL   6'0"   195 lbs.
Position: First Base
New York Giants, Detroit Tigers

G	BA	AB	H	2B	3B	HR	R	RBI	BB	SO	SB	FA
437	.240	1331	320	38	15	51	159	190	106	194	2	.986

A fine minor league hitter, Gail hit .314 for Lenoir in 1950, .339 for Lenoir and Knoxville in 1951, 23 home runs and 93 RBIs for Sioux City in 1952, 25 home runs and 86 RBIs for Nashville in 1953, .309 for Minneapolis in 1954 with 34 home runs and 113 RBIs, and 24 home runs for Minneapolis in 1956. In his rookie year in the big leagues, 1955, he hit 12 home runs in only 263 at-bats with the Giants. Gail was traded with Ozzie Virgil to Detroit in 1958 for Jim Finigan. He hit 20 home runs, eight triples, drove in 83 runs, and batted .273 in 1958 with Detroit, his only season as a full-time player. In 1960 he was traded to the Dodgers for Sandy Amoros.

Gail Harris

When Managers Were Colorful

Back then they allowed the managers to be colorful. Now if a manager steps out of the dugout and says one thing wrong, they kick him out of the game. I mean, some of the greatest shows I've ever seen is Durocher and Jocko Conlin, the little umpire, and they get in a big argument and Durocher kicks on Jocko and Jocko kicks dirt back on Leo. And the fans loved this.

Charlie Grimm, he used to take the visiting team's lineup and he'd bury it on the third base coaching box, when he was coaching, and he'd put black magic all over that thing all day, hexes and all this stuff. But you don't see that any more.

Fred Haney had the Pittsburgh club, and it was so bad he'd just sit over in the corner of the dugout and take Alka-Seltzers and burp all nine innings.

Charlie Grimm was a left-handed banjo player, and he'd get together with a banjo player named Eddie Peabody after the games, and you talk about playing some banjo music. We'd have some good times. But they were more colorful back in those days. Durocher would come out throwing towels, and talking to the umpire, and you'd think he was really cussin' the umpire, and you don't even know what he was talking about.

Paul Richards would walk out of the dugout very calm, one pants leg up and the other down, and he was questioning the umpire's birth from the time he walked out of the dugout 'til he walked back.

There were some colorful managers back then.

Mantle vs. Mays

Gosh, at that time New York had the three best center fielders in baseball. They had Snider with the Dodgers, Mantle, and Mays. If Mickey had good legs—see, he'd tape both those legs every day to play—and I've seen him come down that first base line—he used to bunt a lot with two strikes on him and for base hits—but he'd come down that first base line, you could almost see the tears flying out of his eyes, his legs were hurting so bad, and he would never quit, he was just a tremendous competitor.

Mays could do everything: run, field, throw, hit—loved to play the game. Just loved the game of baseball. Now Mickey abused his body. Mays did not abuse his body. He did not drink. He did not smoke. He took care of himself. And he gave baseball everything that he had.

Art Houtteman

Twelve years (1945-50, 52-57)
Born Aug. 7, 1927 BR TR 6'2" 188 lbs.
Position: Pitcher
Detroit Tigers, Cleveland Indians, Baltimore Orioles

G	W	L	PCT	ERA	GS	CG	SV	IP	H	BB	SO	BA	FA
325	87	91	.489	4.14	181	78	20	1555	1646	516	639	.193	.963

*A*n All-Star in 1950 when he won 19 and saved four games
for the Tigers and pitched a league-leading four shutouts,
*Houtteman lost 20 in 1952 after a year of military service. In 1953
he was traded with Owen Friend, Bill Wight, and Joe Ginsberg to
Cleveland for Ray Boone, Al Aber, Steve Gromek, and Dick Weik.
He went 15-7 and batted .277 with one home run for the pennant-
winning Indians in 1954. He pitched 14 shutouts among his 78
career complete games.*

Sorry, Joe

I had particularly good luck against Joe DiMaggio. I don't know if he looked for more than I had or what. But I had the honor of being named by him as one of the top five pitchers he ever hit against. I had real good luck with him. I think he had something like two doubles, five singles off me—and that's all he ever got off me in probably forty times at bat. He looked bad sometimes, almost to the point I felt guilty. I don't know, he was either looking for something else or—I don't know what. I pitched him the way I had luck against him. I mean, I followed the policy.

The funniest part about that is that the two doubles he got were identical; they were line drives down the left field line in Yankee Stadium. Both of them jumped into the seats on the first bounce, and they were hit—and they were great pitches, low outside, good curve balls, both identical pitches, and he hit them just like they were an echo of each other.

Playing to Hit

I played to hit. Boy, I wouldn't have been a pitcher if I'd been a ballplayer at a time when the pitchers didn't hit here in the American League. I was basically an infielder, outfielder before I was a pitcher. I had good hands, a good arm. I didn't have the speed I needed for the outfield, but I could play third base, or second base. I could hit the ball, but I didn't have the power. My feet got forward too quick. I hit the ball hard, but it wouldn't go far. I was a line drive hitter. But I found out that my quickest way to the big leagues was as a pitcher.

I pinch hit for Al Rosen once and doubled. Now there's something behind that, because he had hit .300 and it was the last day of the season. Had he gone up to bat and made an out, he'd have dropped below three hundred. So they didn't want him to hit. You know, it was a game that didn't mean anything.

Art Houtteman

Sid Hudson

Twelve years (1940-42, 46-54)
Born Jan. 3, 1917   BR   TR   6'4"   180 lbs.
Position: Pitcher
Washington Senators, Boston Red Sox

G	W	L	PCT	ERA	GS	CG	SV	IP	H	BB	SO	BA	FA
380	104	152	.406	4.28	279	123	132	181	2384	835	734	.220	.955

A *two-time All-Star, Hudson won 40 games in his first three years with Washington while completing 55 of 95 starts. After his third season he spent three years in the Army Air Corps and after some arm problems was never the same pitcher. His best season after World War II was 1950, when he went 14-14 with 17 complete games in 30 starts for the Senators. A good hitter, he batted over .200 in eight of his first nine years, including a .308 mark in 1947. Hudson pitched 11 shutouts and two one-hitters, losing one no-hit bid in the ninth inning. In 1952 he was traded to the Red Sox for Randy Gumpert and Walt Masterson. He was a coach with the Senators, Red Sox, and Rangers. He was also a college pitching coach at Baylor University.*

Pitching Debut

I started out in the minors in Sanford, Florida, as a first baseman in 1938. They fired our manager and brought in a new one, and he brought a first baseman with him, so I'm sitting on the bench. A week or so later, we were getting beat pretty bad up in Palatka, Florida, and our manager, Rawmeat Rogers—he got his name Rawmeat from eating raw steaks—he said to me, "You've got a good arm. You ever pitch?"

I said, "Yeah, I've pitched some."

And he said, "Well, you're it."

I went out and pitched the last two innings and struck out the side both innings, and he said, "From now on, you're going to pitch."

So I did. The next year we won the pennant and the playoffs. Altogether, I started 31 games in 1939 and finished all 31. *[In the regular season, Hudson went 24-4 and led the league in strike outs, 190, and ERA, 1.79.]* I went from Class D in 1939 to the majors with Washington in 1940.

Gaylord's Spitter

Gaylord *[Perry]* threw some illegal pitches, but not many. *[Sid Hudson was Perry's pitching coach when Gaylord was with the Texas Rangers.]* He'd go through the rigmarole where he'd touch his cap, his face and his hair and his shirt and everything, but he'd do that on every pitch. He had it on his hair, so he claimed, and he claimed that he could take a swipe at his hair and he'd come down to his shirt and he'd get enough for two pitches. At one time. But he didn't throw it much. He might throw it in a jam once in awhile. It was all more psychological than anything else. He threw hard anyway. He had a good fast ball, a good slider.

I remember one day at Texas, somebody yelled to him from across the way, from one dugout to the other, "Hey, Gaylord, how's your spitter?" He reached in his jacket pocket and pulled out a tube of jelly. So evidently it was all right.

Billy Hunter

Six years (1953-58)
Born June 4, 1928 BR TR 6'0" 180 lbs.
Positions: SS, 528; 2B, 72; 3B, 24
St. Louis Browns, Baltimore Orioles, New York Yankees,
Kansas City Athletics, Cleveland Indians

G	BA	AB	H	2B	3B	HR	R	RBI	BB	SO	SB	FA
630	.219	1875	410	58	18	16	166	144	111	192	23	.960

*H*unter was an All-Star as a Browns rookie in 1953 when he played in all 154 Browns games (Satchel Paige was the other Browns All-Star that year). In November, 1954 he was involved in the first part of an 18-player trade that sent him to the Yankees with Larsen and Turley for Harry Byrd, Jim McDonald, Hal Smith, Gus Triandos, Gene Woodling and Willie Miranda. Two weeks later the trade was completed with nine other players changing teams. Hunter played 98 games at shortstop for the Yankees in 1955, but he didn't play in the World Series—Rizzuto and Jerry Coleman shared the shortstop position. Billy was a longtime coach, and he managed the Texas Rangers in 1977-78. A flashy fielder, his best season at the plate came in 1952 with Fort Worth in the Texas League. He drove in 75 runs, batted .285, and led the league with 24 stolen bases.

Billy Hunter

Pinch-Runner

When I went to the All-Star game in 1953 there were five shortstops on that team. There was Rizzuto, and Carrasquel and Harvey Kuenn and myself and Milt Bolling from the Boston Red Sox. I didn't even take a bat with me.

I pinch ran. For all people to pinch run for, Mickey Mantle was the guy I pinch ran for.

We were down by two runs, and Jim Turner was coaching first base. *[The AL was down 2-0 at the time, lost 5-1.]* There were two men out and he said, "Now your run doesn't mean anything. Don't run into the third out."

On the next pitch Yogi hit a line drive to right field, and I rounded second and slid into third on a bang-bang play. Slaughter had taken the ball on one hop. I was safe, but Turner is over there with his hands up in the air like it was a three-point field goal or a field goal on a football team.

Bill Veeck

Bobo Holloman pitched a no-hitter his first start. It was against the Philadelphia Athletics. One play, Joe Astroth—he was strictly a pull hitter—hit a ground ball up the middle. I went over and dove and caught the ball and threw to first off my knees. Astroth was like Sherm Lollar or most catchers in that he didn't run very fast, so that saved the no-hitter.

Veeck used to wear those open-necked white shirts all the time, so he bought me a dozen shirts because of that play. He was a player's owner. He had his apartment right in the ballpark. He used to come into the clubhouse, and many times he'd come in prior to the game, and take off his wooden leg and throw it in the corner and we'd sit there and play cards on the training table until the team was supposed to report. I enjoyed Bill Veeck.

Strategy

I hit two home runs on one game off Early Wynn, and only hit 16 in my big league career. That particular game we won 4-3 and I drove in all four runs, the fourth one coming in the ninth inning with a 3-3 ballgame with a suicide squeeze. I was with Kansas City and we were playing Cleveland in Kansas City.

My first time up I hit a home run to put us ahead 1-0. They went ahead 2-1 and the next time up I hit a home run with a man on base to put us ahead 3-2 and then they tied it 3-3. And I came to bat the third time in the ninth inning with the bases loaded, and I looked down to the third base coach, Harry Craft, and he's got the suicide squeeze on.

I thought, "He doesn't realize that I had just hit a home run the two times previously at bat." I stepped out of the batter's box and I hit my spikes with my bat. The reason I did that was to acknowledge that I had seen the sign for the squeeze play.

As luck would have it, Early couldn't hit me with the ball, which he would have undoubtedly done since I'd already hit two home runs off of him. Because the bases were loaded and if he hits me the ballgame's over anyway.

So I laid down a perfect bunt down the third base line, and it's like stop action. Al Rosen was the third baseman, Early Wynn's the pitcher, Jim Hegan's the catcher, Hector Lopez is the runner on third and on a suicide squeeze he's supposed to be running home. But he wasn't. But he started to run before anybody else started to go after the ball. And when Rosen and Wynn didn't go after it, Hegan came out from behind the plate.

Lopez passed him on the way in to touch home plate, and I was still in the batter's box when it was all done. And they gave me a hit. I never went to first base. There was one man out, and the ballgame was over.

Phil Rizzuto

Rizzuto was a real gentleman. He was deathly afraid of bugs. Players used to always put something in his sanitary socks or in his glove or whatever. He was kind of the butt of all the clubhouse jokes because of his being afraid of various insects or whatever. You'd see him throwing his sock up in the air or whatever and everybody smiling in the clubhouse. But Phil is a real gentleman, and I was elated when he got into the Hall of Fame.

Randy Jackson

Ten years (1950-59)
Born Feb. 10, 1926 BR TR 6'1 1/2" 180 lbs.
Position: Third Base
Chicago Cubs, Brooklyn Dodgers,
Los Angeles Dodgers, Cleveland Indians

G	BA	AB	H	2B	3B	HR	R	RBI	BB	SO	SB	FA
955	.261	3203	835	115	44	103	412	415	281	382	36	.955

A *two-time All-Star (1954-55), Randy "Handsome Ran-*
*som" Jackson played in two Cotton Bowls as a football
player with TCU. From 1953-55 he hit 19, 19, and 21 home runs
for the Cubs. He was traded to Brooklyn in 1956 to take Jackie
Robinson's place at third base, but became a part-time player after a
knee injury. He appeared three times as a pinch hitter in the 1956
World Series. In his first minor league season, 1948, he hit .322 for
Des Moines of the Western League. In 1949 he hit .298 and drove
in 109 runs for Oklahoma City and led the Texas League with 13
triples. Jackson hit .315 with 20 home runs in 1950 for Springfield
of the International League before coming up to the Cubs.*

Baseball Trivia

I was the last Brooklyn Dodger to hit a home run. I found that out several years ago. I hit it off Don Cardwell. My son called me from down south Georgia and said, "Dad, did you watch *Good Morning, America*?" I said, "No, I didn't. I was shaving." He said, "Well, your name was mentioned. I said, "Why would I be on *Good Morning, America*?" It was a trivia question: "Who was the last Brooklyn Dodger to hit a home run?" He said, "I just happened to be listening to it and your name came up." I said, "That's news to me." *[Jackson hit it off of Don Cardwell.]* I know exactly the date—it happened on 9/27/57. The reason I know that is that I just came from a card show in L.A. and a bunch of folks wanted me to sign my name that way: Ransom Jackson, last Brooklyn Dodger to hit a home run 9/27/57. So I must have signed 20 baseballs with that on there.

And I was at another card show in Chicago and someone said, "Did you know that you're the first ballplayer on record to get an intentional walk?" I said, "You have got to be teasing," because they had intentional walks for about a hundred years. And he said, "No, in the early '50s somebody decided they ought to keep records of intentional walks." So in the year they started keeping records, our game with St. Louis happened to be one of the earlier games, and in the first inning I came up and they walked me intentionally to fill the bases. So those two things are something I've done which nobody else has ever done. You can take that and a quarter down to the coffee shop and maybe get a cup of coffee.

Jackie Robinson's Replacement

The Dodgers got me from the Cubs to take Jackie Robinson's place. This was his last year.

They started the season off with him, and Walter Alston told me he was going to do that, because Jackie had been there so long.

I said, "That's certainly understandable."

He didn't do too well and then they put me in and I started for about three months, two and a half months. I was batting clean-up and driving in runs in just about every game, and just really doing great, like they expected me to. And during All-Star break I was turning a shower off in my apartment in Brooklyn and the porcelain knob broke off in my hand, just ripped my thumb all to pieces, and that was pretty much the end of the season, so I just had to kind of coast from then on, and Jackie came back in and did a good job.

Ernie Banks

Ernie came in '53 and we played side by side two or three years. You knew right away when he came up there that he was going to be great. Of course, he needed some polishing in the infield, but he could just flip those wrists and the ball would just shoot.

So you knew he had it. It was just a matter of getting settled down for a year or so and getting in the groove. And a nice guy. About as nice a guy as you'll find.

Ron Jackson

Seven years (1954-60)
Born Oct. 22, 1933 BR TR 6'7" 225 lbs.
Position: First Base
Chicago White Sox, Boston Red Sox

G	BA	AB	H	2B	3B	HR	R	RBI	BB	SO	SB	FA
196	.245	474	116	18	1	17	54	52	45	119	6	.992

Jackson was signed as a bonus player out of Western Michigan College in 1954 and went directly to the big leagues with no minor league experience. In 1956 he was sent down to Vancouver of the Pacific Coast League where he batted .304 in 82 games. In 1957 he hit .310 with 21 home runs and 102 RBIs for Indianapolis of the American Association. He finished the season with the White Sox, hitting .317 in 13 games. In his years with the White Sox, other White Sox first basemen were Ferris Fain, Walt Dropo, Earl Torgeson, and Ray Boone. He had good power but only once got more than 100 at-bats in a single season (146 in 1958). He made only one error that year in 38 games at first base. In November 1959 he was traded to the Red Sox for Frank Baumann.

Ron Jackson

Not That *Honest*

I hated an umpire who would call you out on strikes and the next time you came up he would say, "I think I missed that one." I really didn't want them to be that honest with me.

Norm Cash

Norm Cash was in the White Sox organization, and he was a pretty good spring hitter. But he played winter ball. He was with the club and then he went down to Indianapolis and I don't think he did particularly well, and then he went and played winter ball, and he come to spring training and he did exceptionally well. That was I think in 1959. He started the season at first base with the White Sox and he played for a little while and then they didn't play him any more. But he started real good.

Well, he goes to winter ball again, and to Cleveland. I got traded to Boston. And when I saw him, it sounded like he was hitting the ball out of a cannon. I mean, everything he hit was loud. And he hit it square.

Then he was traded to Detroit, and he continued on hitting. He went back to winter ball the next year and I think he leads the league in hitting in 1961. Then he couldn't go to winter ball any more and he never got off the dime after that. He hit good later in the season, but he never got that good start again. *[Cash hit .286 in 1960, a league-leading .361 in 1961, and never hit over .283 in his remaining 13 big league seasons.]*

And I attribute it to the fact that he didn't play winter ball again. Some other people might get tired of it, but playing winter ball seemed to work for him.

Spider Jorgensen

Five years (1947-51)
Born Nov. 3, 1919   BL   TR   5'9"   155 lbs.
Position: Third Base (OF, 11)
Brooklyn Dodgers, New York Giants

G	BA	AB	H	2B	3B	HR	R	RBI	BB	SO	SB	FA
267	.266	755	201	40	11	9	97	107	106	75	5	.941

*Jorgensen was the Dodgers' starting third baseman in 1947 on
an infield that had Reese at short, Stanky at second, and Jackie
Robinson at first. He hit .274 that season and played all seven games in
the Dodgers' World Series loss to the Yankees. In 1948 he hit .300 in an
injury-shortened 31-game season. In 1949 he played 53 games for the
Dodgers and four more games in the World Series. An arm injury shortened his career.*

The Nickname

I come from Folsom, a little town outside of Sacramento. It's a big town now. When I was going to high school, we'd have this scrimmage basketball game in gym period, the skins against the shirts. This one day I was on the skins, no jersey, and I always wore a pair of black trunks with an orange stripe running down the side. We're scrimmaging up and down the floor, and one of the other coaches came in and said, "Who's that skinny little fart over there, with those orange and black trunks on?"

The other coach said, "Oh, that's one of the Jorgensen guys."

The first coach said, "Well, he looks just like that black widow spider that I uncovered under my lumber pile out in the backyard last Friday."

So the name stuck. In those days, it seemed like everybody had a lumber pile out in back, so when you'd have to do odd jobs around the house, you'd just go out to the lumber pile. About once a month, or every two months, you'd have to go out and rearrange that pile, and there'd always be black widow spiders in those things. You had to be careful. But that's how the thing originated.

The players that I played with earlier in my career called me Spider all the time. But at Montreal and when I first went to Brooklyn it was Johnny. They just ask you your first name, and it's "John" and that's it. It wasn't until later that when my buddies, like Bruce Edwards, called me Spider that it caught on with the reporters and announcers.

Spider Jorgensen

Ted Kazanski

Six years (1953-58)
Born Jan. 25, 1934   BR   TR   6'1"   175 lbs.
Positions: 2B, 197; SS, 163; 3B, 56
Philadelphia Phillies

G	BA	AB	H	2B	3B	HR	R	RBI	BB	SO	SB	FA
417	.217	1329	288	49	9	14	118	163	90	163	4	.966

A highly regarded prospect, Kazanski played 88 games in the Three-I League in 1951 with Terre Haute at the age of 17. The following year he hit .254 with 10 home runs for Schenectady of the Easter League. In 1953 he hit .290 in 60 games for Baltimore of the International League before coming up with the Phillies and playing 95 games at shortstop for them. He played over 100 games only one year in the big leagues, 1956. His career ended in 1958 at the age of 24.

A Bunch of Kids

The day I broke into the Majors—late June of 1953—Wrigley Field in Chicago, 19 years old—just up from Baltimore—and scared to death.

I was lead-off man in the lineup. Pitching for the Cubs was Howie Pollet and catching, Joe Garagiola. Kiner and Sauer in the outfield—guys I had only read about, and now we were playing on the same field.

It was a beautiful, sunny June day, and I can still see the beautiful ivy on the outfield walls and smell the cigar smoke, and hear the sounds that make a ballpark special.

Pat Piper was the P.A. announcer—a little guy in a Panama hat, who sat on a stool right on the field against the backstop. As he announced, "Number seven for the Phillies" I walked into the batter's box on legs of Jello. Here it was—the culmination of a lifelong dream—"I'm in the Majors"—and proceeded to strike out on three pitches! Welcome to the Majors!

The rest of the day, however, was great. We won the game and I did manage to help by getting three hits.

I used to love to go to the ballpark. We'd go out four or five hours before the game, strip down to our shorts, get a chew of tobacco, light up a nice cigar and have a great time just talking and fooling around like a bunch of kids, which I guess we were.

Skeeter Kell

One year (1952)
Born Oct. 11, 1929 BR TR 5'9" 160 lbs.
Position: Second Base
Philadelphia Athletics

G	BA	AB	H	2B	3B	HR	R	RBI	BB	SO	SB	FA
75	.221	213	47	8	3	0	24	17	14	18	5	.963

Brother of Hall-of-Fame third baseman George, Skeeter played in just one big league season, sharing second-base duties with Cass Michaels and Pete Suder. That fourth-place Athletics team also had Ferris Fain, Eddie Joost, Hank Majeski, and Billy Hitchock in the infield. Outfielders were Elmer Valo, Dave Philley, and Gus Zernial. Joe Astroth did the catching, and Bobby Shantz was the staff's pitching ace and American League MVP.

Family Competition

George's family *[brother George Kell]*, all drove from Detroit, and our mother and dad drove from Arkansas to see us play against each other in Philadelphia. The Tigers played in Washington the night before we were going to play against each other, and Dad and I went to the train station at midnight to pick George up. When he got off the train he said, "Skeet, we won't be playing against each other tomorrow."

I said "Why?"

He said, "I know I'm fixin' to be traded. I didn't play tonight. The rumor is I'm going to the Red Sox."

The next day was the last day of the trading deadline. About three o'clock in the afternoon our phone rang at the house and George and Charlene and all his family and my wife and son and mother and daddy were out riding around looking at where George and Charlene lived when they lived in Philadelphia. Johnny Lipon called me and said that he and George and some others had been traded to the Red Sox and they were supposed to catch a plane out at five-thirty that afternoon and play at Boston that night. But George didn't get back in 'til almost five, so he didn't go until the next day. He sat in the stands that night; Mother and Dad never did get to see us play against each other. *[Kell, Dizzy Trout, Lipon and Hoot Evers went to Boston for Walt Dropo, Bill Wight, Fred Hatfield, Johnny Pesky, and Don Lenhardt.]*

Skeeter Kell

Ralph Kiner

Ten years (1946-55)
Born October 27, 1922 BR TR 6'2" 195 lbs.
Positions: OF, 1382; 1B, 58
Pittsburgh Pirates, Chicago Cubs, Cleveland Indians

G	BA	AB	H	2B	3B	HR	R	RBI	BB	SO	SB	FA
1472	.279	5205	1451	216	39	369	971	1015	1011	749	22	.975

*K*iner was elected to Baseball's Hall of Fame in 1975. One of baseball's all-time great sluggers, he led the National League in home runs his first seven seasons. He hit 40 or more home runs five years in a row, scoring and driving in more than 100 runs each season. During his 10-year career his season averages were 37 home runs, 101 RBIs, and 101 walks. In June, 1953 he was traded with Joe Garagiola, Howie Pollet and Catfish Metkovich from the Pirates to the Cubs for six players and cash. Kiner's ratio of homer to at bats is second only to Babe Ruth on the all-time list. He was a six-time All-Star and was* The Sporting News' *Player of the Year in 1950. A bad back forced his retirement at the age of 33. Beginning in 1962, Kiner was a longtime broadcaster.*

Hitting Out of the White Shirts

Wrigley Field wasn't an easy park to hit in. In those days it was very tough, because they had the people sitting in center field, and the ball came out of the white shirts. Everybody forgets about that. It was an extremely difficult ballpark to hit in. You could never find the ball because of the people in the white shirts.

While I was there, I was the player representative for the National League, and we finally got it blocked out. I believe the year was '54, but I'm not sure. That opened it up to being a much better hitter's park. It all depended on which way the wind blew. In the early part of the year and latter part of the year it blew in most of the time. That made it somewhat difficult.

Contract Battle

I thought Branch Rickey was a brilliant man. And at the same time, he's probably the man who created the worst situation you could have for a baseball player. He was extremely difficult to deal with, and probably brought on the union more than anything else. I thought he was extremely intelligent, and at the same time he was for Branch Rickey and did not care at all for any of the people who played underneath him, although he may have seemed to because he was a brilliant orator.

I had a very vitriolic battle with him in 1953. I had led the league in home runs with 37 and he cut my salary 25 percent, and I held out against the cut. We exchanged communications back and forth, and I refused to sign the 25 percent cut, which was the maximum cut. I was the only reason why they were drawing any people there. And finally he came out to Hollywood. We met— their farm club was the Hollywood Stars, and they played on a field called Gilmore Field in Hollywood. And I met him there in the office of Bob Cox, who was the owner of the Brown Derby Restaurant and the owner of the Hollywood Stars baseball team.

I said, "I'm not going to take the 25 percent cut."

He said, "Where'd we finish?"

I said, "We finished last," and he said, "We can finish last without you." I either took it, or I didn't play. Out of that meeting I finally agreed to take the 25 percent cut, and part of the deal was that I didn't have to go the first two weeks of spring training in Havana, Cuba, where we were training at the time. Those two weeks were the two weeks you got in shape, and then the games started. I agreed that I'd show up for the games.

This was a verbal agreement. Then he told the press that I was demanding that I got special accommodations and special travel, and I demanded the fence should not be lengthened. They were all lies. That's why I have no personal regard for him, because he lied to the press, he lied to me. At the same time it served his purpose.

Nellie King

Four years (1955-57)
Born Mar. 15, 1928 BR TR 6'6" 185 lbs.
Position: Pitcher
Pittsburgh Pirates

G	W	L	PCT	ERA	GS	CG	SV	IP	H	BB	SO	BA	FA
95	7	5	.583	3.58	4	0	6	173.1	193	50	72	.000	1.000

King pitched all but four of his 95 games for the Pirates in relief before his career was shortened by arm trouble. He had outstanding control. In almost 1,500 major- and minor league innings pitched, he averaged fewer than two and a half walks per nine innings. In his final two seasons with the Pirates he appeared in 74 games in relief with a 6-2 record and six saves. He batted 23 times for the Pirates without a hit and fielded 39 chances without an error. King won 20 games in 1948 for New Iberia in the Evangeline. League while pitching a league-leading 284 innings. In 1953 with Denver, after two years of military service, he led the Western League in games pitched (50) and in winning percentage (.833); he won 15 and lost three. In 1954 with New Orleans of the Southern Association he went 16-5 and led the league with a 2.25 ERA. He broadcast the Pittsburgh Pirate games for nine seasons.

Dale Long

Dale Long set a record with home runs in eight consecutive games in 1956. I was fortunate to be the recipient of two wins during that streak. I won only seven in my brief major league career), so I can relate to that record well. *[King was 4-1 with five saves that season in 38 games.]*

Two incidents during that streak come to mind. The first was a Friday night game at Connie Mack Stadium in Philly. I had come on in relief in the fourth inning or so and pitched well, going four plus innings to pick up the win. Long homered and the streak reached six consecutive games. After the game the media congregated around Long's locker. The rest of us were waiting on the team bus after showering. Some of the players were anxious to get back to the hotel as we had a day game the next day.

Someone hollered from the back of the bus, "Who are we waiting for?"

I said, "Long. All the media is interested in his home run streak."

Someone replied, "To hell with him, let him get a cab."

I stepped out the door of the bus, "Dale Long has carried us this far and this bus isn't leaving without Dale Long." I went out and laid down on the street in front of the bus and said the same thing. All of this drew a great laugh from the players and admiration from Dale Long.

Long tied the record the next day in Philly. We got rained out on Sunday and had an off day on Monday before returning to action on Tuesday against the Dodgers on, I believe, May 28, 1956. This gave the media a lot of time to do stories on Dale Long and his chance to set the consecutive home run record at home, at Forbes Field.

As I recall we had an almost sellout crowd that night. Carl Erskine was pitching for the Dodgers and Long failed to hit a homer his first time up. His second time up he hit one and it brought the crowd (and the Pirate players in the dugout and bullpen) to their feet, cheering and clapping. Long circled the bases and entered the dugout. The crowd remained standing and cheering and clapping.

Then something happened that had never taken place before in baseball history. The fans, still on their feet cheering and clapping, would not allow the game to continue until Dale Long took a curtain call. According to Branch Rickey, who began his major league career in 1913 as manager of the St. Louis Cardinals, it was the first time he had seen or heard of a hitter being requested by the fans to take a curtain call. Today hitters are taking curtain calls in some parks for hitting a double in the fourth inning.

Dale Long was one of the truly great persons I had the privilege of playing with. He was a leader. We were in first place in the NL in mid-June of 1956 due to his hitting and leadership. Looking back I think Dale really was the key in turning the Pirates from a young team that was unsure it could win, to one that *knew* it could. That team in 1956 was the nucleus of the 1960 World Championship team with players such as Clemente, Groat, Mazerowski, Skinner, Virdon, Friend, Law, Face and others. *[Long was traded from the Pirates in 1957.]* Tragically Dale died at an early age a few years ago *[in 1991, at the age of 64]* of cancer.

Roberto Clemente

Roberto Clemente had tremendous pride and confidence in his ability to perform in clutch moments. He made what I think was the greatest catch I saw in my years of playing and broadcasting major league baseball. I was broadcasting Pirates games with Bob Prince. I think the year was 1970 or 1971. We were leading the Astros in Houston in the eighth inning by a run with two out and the tying run at second and Bob Watson at bat. Watson hit a drive down the right field line, slicing away from Clemente. It looked like a sure double and possibly a home run. Somehow Clemente caught up with the ball just as it was about to hit the fence. He reached up, it looked like his glove was above the yellow line, hit the fence face first, fell to the ground and held up his glove to indicate he still held the ball. It was a game-saving catch.

On the way back to the hotel on the team bus I sat next to Roberto and told him I thought that was the best catch I had ever seem him make. He turned to me and said proudly, "Nellie, I will tell you something. If the game is on the line and the ball is in the park, I will catch the ball."

Roberto was a very proud man and had more depth to him as a human being than any player I have met in my lifetime. The closest I could compare with him would be Michael Jordan.

Bill Mazerowski

Mazerowski was a brilliant player, a very intelligent kid. He knew the game, because he played with older people. He was like 14, 15, playing with guys that were 18 and 20 years old.

He wasn't exceptionally fast, but he had quick feet and he knew how to play hitters. He knew what the score was. He was always telling me, "If there's a tying run at second base, I never let a ground ball go through to center field. I always made sure I got it because that would hold a runner at third. But if it went to my left, to right field, I knew Clemente would throw him out."

I think Mazerowski should be in the Hall of Fame. *[He was elected to the Hall of Fame in 2001 by the Veteran's Committee.]* He wasn't a bad hitter. He batted eighth most of his career. And you know, you're not going to put stats on the board there. You're not going to see much to hit batting eighth, with the pitcher coming up. But he still batted around .265, .270. *[His lifetime average was .260; in his first 10 seasons, he hit .265 or better seven times.]*

I think his first full year he hit something like 17, 18 home runs. *[He hit eight in 1957, his first full season, then 19 in 1958; he never hit more than 16 after that.]* And they changed him, tried to get him to hit the ball all over the place. But I don't think I've ever seen a player better than him in clutch situations.

Playing for Danny Murtaugh

I thought Murtaugh was the best manager I ever played for. I played for him in the minor leagues. He was the kind of guy, in those days, if you got into trouble as a pitcher he'd come out to the mound, and he'd never take you out if you got into trouble early. He wanted you to work out of it because if you keep yanking guys about the third or fourth inning, they start looking over their shoulder, you know? They lose their confidence, and I think he understood that because he was not a great major league player. *[He hit .254 in nine big league seasons.]* He knew what the average player was like. He knew that they had to gain confidence, and by gaining confidence he let them do the things that he knew they could do, but let them prove it to themselves.

In 1957 he took over as manager with the Pirates when Bragan left and Clyde Sukeforth turned the job down. Danny was the coach there and he became the interim manager. The first night we had a clubhouse meeting, and he didn't say much, just about how you'd play the hitters and stuff.

In about two weeks—he never had any clubhouse meetings—and after two weeks he said, "You know, everybody's wondering when I was going to have a clubhouse meeting. I don't like to do a lot of talking, but I do a lot of listening and I do a lot of watching. I've been watching and listening the last two weeks, and I've got some things I want to say." And he said them.

He was very strong. I think that good managers are great fathers, because good fathers know their kids. They never will embarrass them. They always put them in positions where they have a chance to succeed. They have confidence in them. They trust them. And he did that.

Johnny Klippstein

Eighteen years (1950-67)
Born Oct. 17, 1927   BR   TR   6'1"   173 lbs.
Position: Pitcher
Chicago Cubs, Cincinnati Reds, Los Angeles Dodgers,
Cleveland Indians, Washington Senators, Philadelphia Phillies,
Minnesota Twins, Detroit Tigers

G	W	L	PCT	ERA	GS	CG	SV	IP	H	BB	SO	BA	FA
711	101	118	.461	4.24	162	37	66	1967.2	1915	978	1158	.125	.966

*K*lippstein pitched professionally from 1944 to 1967. In 1965 he joined with Al Worthington in the Minnesota Twins' bullpen to help the Twins win the AL pennant. He pitched 56 games in relief that year, going 9-3 with five saves and a 2.24 ERA. With Cleveland in 1960 he appeared in 49 games with a 2.91 ERA, going 5-5 with a league-leading 14 saves. In 1963 he had a 1.93 ERA for the Phillies in 49 games. In 1958 he was traded with Steve Bilko from the Reds to the Dodgers for Don Newcombe. From 1958-64 he pitched for six different teams. Fifty-nine of his 101 big league wins came in relief. During his first eight seasons he pitched both as a starter and reliever, but in his last 10 seasons only 13 of his last 396 appearances were starts.

A Good Time Not to Pinch Hit

We were playing in Houston in 1962. I was playing for Fred Hutchinson. I think Bob Purkey pitched the first 10 innings down there, and it was a nothing-nothing ballgame. And of course the heat in Houston was pretty bad. This was before they moved into the Astrodome.

I went in to the pitch the 11th. I pitched the 11th and 12th, and it was still nothing-nothing at the end of the 12th. Hutch was going to pinch hit for me in the top of the 13th. The second guy made an out and Joe Gaines, who was in the on-deck circle to pinch hit, was called back. *[Gaines went 12-40 as a pinch hitter for the Reds that year.]*

I went up to hit, and Joe Gaines handed me his bat, which was a little old 34 inch, about a 31 ounce bat, which was a lighter and shorter than I was using.

He said, "It's got good wood in it, John. Use it."

So Don McMahon threw me a high slider. I didn't think I could hit the ball 410 feet, but I hit it over the left center field fence. I can remember rounding second base, and Bob Aspromonte, who was playing third, had his hands on his hips and was shaking his head, and I told him I was just surprised as he was.

So anyway, that was the only run we got, 1-0, and I got them out in the bottom of the 13th, and we win 1-0 in 13 innings. So that had to be one of my biggest thrills.

A Key to Longevity

I played about 18 years in the big leagues, and I pitched five in the minors, and of course I was in the service one year, where I played about 80-some games then too. I really felt like the secret to pitching a long time was doing a lot of running, and throwing in between starts at the right time, and just keeping your arm strong if you could. I think Johnny Sain probably had that down to a science. He said that lot of pitchers fool themselves where they think they're getting their arm in shape, and they really are not throwing enough. And sometimes they come up with bad arms, or tired arms, because they get in a situation where they're throwing a lot over a short period of time, and their arm is not really in shape. So his theory was to throw every day in spring training, even if it's just ten minutes.

He said, "First you have to get your arm strong. Once you get your arm strong, then you have to take care of it. You have to warm up properly, gotta make sure you give it the rest between starts. A lot of running. Exercises with repetitions, not necessarily weights."

Johnny Sain was a great pitching coach, because he never was overbearing. He always planted a thought and kind of worked his way in slowly. He walked by and saw you throwing a pitch and said, "Hey, looks pretty good, you're doing a good job with that." And he'd keep on walking. He was planting the seed.

Or he'd say, "Well, why don't you just try it on the side a little bit?" Pretty soon he had you throwing it. He was pretty clever, rather than coming up, "Hey, you can't do this, you have to do this this way." He didn't approach it that way. So he worked very well with pitchers.

Nothing to This Game

In my first game of pro ball, I pitched three innings in relief and I struck out five out of nine. They didn't hit a ball out of the infield, and of course all the guys and the manager were patting me on the back.

Then I went out the next five or six times I got in a ball game and I couldn't get anybody out. Either I couldn't get the ball over the plate or when I did they hit it. That's when I was sent to a Class D team in Lima, Ohio.

But that first day I said, "Boy, there's nothing to this pro ball."

Playing for Alston and Tebbetts

Walter Alston was a quiet man who got things done by saying very little, but everybody had great respect for him, and I think he had great knowledge of handling a pitching staff. And I think that was most of his success, was being able to handle people and keep them in line and keep everybody happy, and also being able to handle a pitching staff.

I think that Birdie Tebbetts, on the other hand, was a great psychologist. He had a way with people. I remember in '56 when we almost won the pennant, we finished two games out. He had a meeting with the pitchers before the season started, and he said, "Well, fellows, I don't care what the newspapers write, we've got a better pitching staff than what they say, and we can win this thing because you guys would run through the wall for me."

What we didn't know was about three weeks later he called all the hitters in—infielders, outfielders, and catchers—and said, "Fellows, you know what kind of a pitching staff we have. We're going to have to score a lot of runs."

We ended up having a pretty good ballclub that year. We came up a little short, but we came within two games of winning the damn thing. But he was a pretty good guy to play for. I thought he was a ballplayer's manager.

Bob Kuzava

Ten years (1946-47, 49-55, 57)
Born May 28, 1923 BB TL 6'2" 202 lbs.
Position: Pitcher
Cleveland Indians, Chicago White Sox, Washington Senators,
New York Yankees, Baltimore Orioles, Philadelphia Phillies,
Pittsburgh Pirates, St. Louis Cardinals

G	W	L	PCT	ERA	GS	CG	SV	IP	H	BB	SO	BA	FA
213	49	44	.527	4.05	99	34	13	862	849	415	446	.086	.942

*I*n *1942 Kuzava led the Middle Atlantic League with 21 wins for Charleston, then he spent three years in the military, where he rose to rank of sergeant. He reached the big leagues with Cleveland in 1946 and was traded to the White Sox in 1948. He won 10 games for the White Sox in 1949 and 11 for the Senators and Yankees in 1951. He was traded with Cass Michaels and John Ostrowski from the White Sox to the Senators in 1950 for Al Kozar, Ray Scarborough and Eddie Robinson. In 1951 he was traded from the Senators to the Yankees for Fred Sanford, Tom Ferrick and Bob Porterfield. Twenty-three of his 49 wins came with the Yankees between 1951-54. He pitched in the 1951, '52, and '53 World*

Series, saving the final game of the '51 and '52 Series. He was used mostly as a reliever in his last four seasons, with 69 of his last 87 appearances coming in relief. In one of his six starts in 1953 he lost a no-hit bid in the ninth inning. Kuzava pitched seven shutouts in his 99 big league starts.

To New York on Crutches

When the Yankees traded for me on June 15 of 1951, I was on crutches. About 10 days before, in Washington, I had been injured in a game against the White Sox. It was a double play, where the pitcher comes over to first. Our first baseman fielded the ball—Mickey Vernon—a ground ball by Nellie Fox with a man on first. Vernon threw to the shortstop to get the lead man, then I came over on first base to get the throw from the shortstop. Fox just happened to step on my heel. He flipped, and there I am with a nicked Achilles and a compound sprain.

So now I'm coming to the park every day for whirlpool, and I'm on crutches. It had to be eight to 10 days that I had been on crutches. So Mr. Griffith, who they called "the Old Fox," traded me over to the Yankees on crutches for four ballplayers and a hundred thousand dollars. I couldn't believe the old man traded me, being in that condition, you know. But he did, and George Weiss went along with it. Bob Porterfield, Freddie Sanford, Tom Ferrick, and a minor leaguer named Snyder and a hundred grand for me, and I'm on crutches!

George Weiss, the Yankees' general manager, called me up and said, "Glad to have you. Come on over here and pitch one of the Sunday games."

I said, "I can't pitch for you." He thought I was kidding.

He said, "What do you mean?" This was on Friday, the 15th.

I said, "I'm on crutches."

He said, "You've gotta be kidding me!"

Bob Kuzava

I said, "No, why would I kid you?"

I was living with my wife and children in Maryland then, about 25 miles from Griffith Stadium, a place called Silver Springs, Maryland. I said, "I got to take my family home, and I'll come to New York and join the club as soon as I get them settled."

He says, "Well, what happened?"

Can you believe that a ballclub like the New York Yankees would trade for a pitcher and give that kind of money and I'm on crutches?

He said, "Well, you go do what you have to do and get over here."

I went into New York on crutches, and there were about four doctors there checking me out. He really could have called it no trade, because I was damaged goods. I couldn't even walk fast. Jim Turner, the pitching coach, knew I was a starter; that's what they got me for, to be the fourth starter, along with Reynolds, Raschi, and Lopat, because Ford was in the service for a year. So, he says, "What you do is just go in the outfield before the game and walk, try to jog a little. We'll put you in the bullpen. When we're way ahead we'll bring you in, when we're way behind we'll bring you in. When your arm's ready to pitch we'll get you some innings."

I did that, and I had a hell of a year. *[Kuzava was 8-4 with five saves.]* I would spot start, if we had a lot of games, doubleheaders and that, or if I was good against some ballclubs Turner would pitch me, like against the Philadelphia A's and Washington Senators. They never could beat me, I don't know why. You just had a hex on some clubs.

Yankee Catchers

Houk and Silvera didn't get much playing time, backing up Yogi Berra. Naturally they wanted to play. But I would imagine those two guys could have probably caught with other ballclubs if they hadn't have been with the Yankees, yet they knew that just about every year they were going to get a World Series paycheck. When we played, $15,000 was a lot of money in salary, then you picked up an extra $6,000, $7,000 or $8,000 World Series check if you won, and that was nearly half of what you made for the whole year. That was pretty good money, and I figured they were happy doing the job they were doing because some other ballclub they might have made eleven or thousand dollars catching, but there would have been no World Series check.

You know, you weren't going to catch ahead of Yogi. The only time we used those guys was in a doubleheader, during the summer when it got pretty hot. They were good big league catchers, but there's only one Yogi Berra, one Roy Campanella, one Johnny Bench. They worked hard every day they were in the bullpen warming up the pitchers. Mechanically they were good catchers and they knew how to call a ballgame, and they didn't get to the Yankees by being bad ballplayers or bad hitters.

Hustle

I was with the White Sox when Nellie Fox came to us from the Philadelphia A's. He was a reserve when I was over at the White Sox. Later on, when I pitched against him, he was tough. He liked to drag the ball, bunt, and you had to be careful, and you'd bring that third-baseman in and a lot of times he'd try to slap the ball by the third baseman.

Nellie was tough with the bat because he had good bat control and he used a big bottle bat, and you'd get him two strikes and he wouldn't strike out because he'd just try to get the wood on the ball. You'd play him in, the outfielder would play him in, because he didn't hit the long ball, but once in awhile he'd unload.

He was a little hustler. He didn't have a lot of natural ability, but I'll tell you, he busted his butt on every play. There were guys with more ability than Nelson Fox, but they didn't apply themselves and they didn't hustle like he did. The guy made himself a pretty good ballplayer.

Jim Landis

Eleven years (1957-67)
Born Mar. 9, 1934 BR TR 6'1" 180 lbs.
Position: Outfield
Chicago White Sox, Kansas City Athletics, Cleveland Indians,
Houston Astros, Detroit Tigers, Boston Red Sox

G	BA	AB	H	2B	3B	HR	R	RBI	BB	SO	SB	FA
1346	.247	4288	1061	169	50	93	625	467	588	767	139	.989

*L*andis was an All-Star in 1962 and a Gold Glove winner *for five straight years (1960-64). In 1961 he had his career highs in batting average (.283), home runs (22) and RBIs (85). He played center field for the White Sox for the first eight of his 11 big league seasons. At the time of his retirement, his fielding average was second highest all-time among outfielders. In the six-game 1959 World Series against the Los Angeles Dodgers, he hit .292 and scored six of his team's 23 runs.*

The First Game

Playing my first big league game was my biggest dream come true.

Since I was seven years old I had a bat in my hands and only thoughts of baseball.

In my first game my main thought was, "Wow! I sure hope every pitcher isn't this tough." It was Herb Score.

Nellie Fox

Nellie Fox—there's a great leader of great people. And a great person he was. There would be no doubt he'd be in the Hall of Fame; to me that's the kind of character that should be there. As a good ballplayer, also. I was totally amazed what great stats he had overall for his career. He was just a tremendous person. He was the best quiet leader on a baseball field you could have.

Nellie got creamed once at second base by Bob Cerv. I mean, Cerv practically killed him. We went out to dinner that night—we knew that he couldn't even move then. So he put on the uniform the next day and played I think four or five innings and finally had to be taken out because he couldn't even move, he was so sore. But that was a tribute to Nellie's toughness and desire.

Jim Landis

Max Lanier

Fourteen years (1938-46, 49-53)
Born Aug. 18, 1915   BR   TL   5'11"   180 lbs.
Position: Pitcher
St. Louis Cardinals, New York Giants, St. Louis Browns

G	W	L	PCT	ERA	GS	CG	SV	IP	H	BB	SO	BA	FA
327	108	82	.568	3.01	204	91	17	1618.1	1490	611	821	.185	.959

*L*anier was a two-time All-Star (1943-44). He pitched 21 career shutouts. He won a total of 45 games for the three consecutive pennant-winning Cardinal teams of 1942-44. He was 6-0 in 1946 with a 1.90 ERA when he jumped to the Mexican League, causing his suspension from organized baseball. Reinstated in 1949, he won 11 games for the Cardinals in both 1950 and 1951. In seven World Series games, he was 2-1 with a 1.71 ERA in 31 $^2/_3$ innings. Lanier won game four of the 1942 Series and the sixth (the decisive) game of the 1944 Series. His son Hal was a major league player, coach, and manager.

Bird Dogs

I got two bird dogs for signing my first contract in 1934. I was a quail hunter, and Frank Rickey, a scout for the Cardinals, came down, and I signed it. I took those bird dogs the next day, and I thought they were ready to hunt, and gosh, one of them got out the first night and I never saw it again. That was my bonus for signing.

I signed at Greensboro, North Carolina, for $100 a month. That was Class B ball then. I was there I guess a week or ten days and they wanted to send me to Huntington, West Virginia, for $70 a month in the Class D league, and I quit.

Nineteen thirty-seven was my first full year in professional ball. I played for Columbus. We won the pennant that year and I won 10 and lost four, and won one in the Little World Series. We had a good ball club. We had Slaughter and Mort Cooper and Johnny Rizzo and Skeeter Webb—we had eight guys that went to the big leagues the next year. *[Slaughter led the league in batting with a .382 average. Rizzo had a 36-game hitting streak. Columbus pitcher Max Macon led the league with 21 wins. Columbus pitcher Bill McGee led the league with a 2.97 ERA.]*

Danny Gardella

Danny Gardella was a colorful ballplayer. I had a barnstorming tour in '48. He was with us and we were playing in Louisiana. He was playing center field. We had a big lead, and there was a big flagpole in center field and we looked out there and he was halfway up the flagpole while the game was going on.

Bob Lennon

Three years (1954, 56-57)
Born Sept. 15, 1928 BL TL 6'0" 200 lbs.
Position: Outfield
New York Giants, Chicago Cubs

G	BA	AB	H	2B	3B	HR	R	RBI	BB	SO	SB	FA
38	.165	79	13	2	0	1	5	4	5	26	0	.900

*B*ob had one of the greatest minor league seasons in history
with Nashville of the Southern Association in 1954 (64
home runs, 161 RBIs, 139 runs scored, 210 hits, and a .345 batting average). He hit 31 home runs with 104 RBIs with Minneapolis of the American Association in 1955. (Six more home runs in the
playoffs helped Minneapolis to the Little World Series crown.) In
1960 he helped lead Montreal to the International League pennant, with 28 home runs and 89 RBIs. He stole 19 bases in his first
full season in the minors, 1946. He played nine years in the minors
before getting a shot at the majors. His major league career was cut
short by arm trouble (a pinched nerve). Bob was traded with Dick
Littlefield from the Giants to the Cubs in 1957 for Ray Jablonski
and Ray Katt.

Willie Mays

You play with Willie Mays or guys of that caliber, definitely they stand out. I was playing right field in Ebbets Field one day and I went to make a catch in right center field and at the last minute he called me off and Geez, I had to dive and roll out of the way to keep from running into him. Don Mueller said when I come in, "Boy, if you ever ran into him they would have sent you out to Podunk."

How to Lose a Pitcher

One day in Jacksonville our manager had a big snake he killed—I guess it was a rattlesnake—and he had him covered over with a burlap bag at home plate. We had a big lefthanded pitcher, Dean Lampros, and the manager said to pick up the snake and chase him.

I went running after him with the snake, and I threw it, and Geez, it wrapped around his neck a little—it was dead, of course, but the poor guy almost had a heart attack.

Don Liddle

Four years (1953-56)
Born May 25, 1925 BL TL 5'10" 165 lbs.
Position: Pitcher
Milwaukee Braves, New York Giants, St. Louis Cardinals

G	W	L	PCT	ERA	GS	CG	SV	IP	H	BB	SO	BA	FA
117	28	18	.609	3.75	54	13	4	427.2	397	203	198	.152	.946

*D*on pitched three shutouts for the World Champion New York Giants in 1954. He started and won the final game of the 1954 World Series against Cleveland, 7-4, yielding just one earned run in seven innings. In the Series' first game, he threw the pitch to Vic Wertz on which Willie Mays made his memorable catch. Fifty-four of his games were as a starter, 67 as reliever. He was traded to New York with Johnny Antonelli in 1954 for Bobby Thomson. He was part of the eight-player trade between the Giants and Cardinals in 1956 involving Schoendienst and Dark.

Pitching at Ebbets and the Polo Grounds

The Polo Grounds, good Lord, it was 90 miles to center field, right center, left center, so to throw the long fly ball in the Polo Grounds presented no problem. But Ebbets Field wouldn't hold them. You had to make them hit the ball on the ground if you could. Right field was terribly, terribly close in Ebbets Field. With a high screen.

Now down the lines in the Polo Grounds were short. What hurt you the most in the Polo Grounds is somebody that hit the ball to the opposite field and it curved toward the foul line. If they hit it very good it'd hit against the wall or curve up into the stands because it was close right down the line. It went out so fast that it didn't give you a whole lot of trouble if you threw fly balls to center field.

Leo Durocher vs. Charlie Grimm

I enjoyed Durocher. He was tough, and he got on you. If you made a mistake he let you know about it, but he didn't harp on it. The next day you were in his good graces, he put his arm around you and he'd forget about it. But he wanted to tell you for sure when you made a mistake, that you realized that you made a mistake, that you threw to the wrong base or you didn't cover first base on a ground ball to the first baseman, or you made a bad pitch, or you weren't backing up this. Anything you might do out there on the mound, when you made a mistake, he told you about it. He told you in a loud, rough way. He wanted it to stick.

But as I say, he didn't harp on it anymore. He said his piece and it was all over with. I enjoyed him. I thought he was a good manager, he got a lot out of a ballplayer.

Don Liddle

His style was completely different from Charlie Grimm's. Charlie Grimm was easygoing, wouldn't raise his voice. Charlie talked to you about mistakes, also. Sometimes attempting bunts, you'd try to beat it out—you tried to drag instead of bunting the man over, sacrificing. You'd try to get a base hit out of it, and Charlie would say something to you about it, but in a nice, easy way. Leo would raise his voice and scream a little bit. He didn't want a base hit, he wanted a sacrifice.

They were completely different in personality. But I liked both of them as managers.

Danny Litwhiler

Eleven years (1940-44, 46-51)
Born Aug. 31, 1916 BR TR 5'10 $^1/_2$" 198 lbs.
Position: Outfield (3B, 20)
Philadelphia Phillies, St. Louis Cardinals,
Boston Braves, Cincinnati Reds

G	BA	AB	H	2B	3B	HR	R	RBI	BB	SO	SB	FA
1057	.281	3494	982	162	32	107	428	451	299	377	11	.981

*An All-Star in 1942, Litwhiler was traded to the Cardi-
nals in 1943 with Earl Naylor and played in the 1943
and '44 World Series with the Cardinals. As a rookie with the Phillies
in 1940, he hit .345 in 36 games. In his first full season, 1941, he
hit .305 with a career-high 18 home runs. Knee injuries severely
hampered his career, and after 1944 he played in a hundred games
only twice. In 1942 he became the first outfielder in history to play
at least 150 games without an error. In 1943 he had only one error
in 116 games. He was a longtime college baseball coach for Florida
State and Michigan State Universities.*

Retaliation

My first year up, I faced Ace Adams in the Polo Grounds. *[Adams led the NL in games pitched in 1942, '43, and '44.]* Hank Danning was the catcher *[Danning caught for the Giants from 1933-42, his entire career, and hit .285]*. I was on second base and I was trying to score on a single. They got me out pretty much, maybe by ten feet, and Danning's got the ball in the baseline, standing straight up here, right in front of the plate, and I thought, "There's only one thing to do, is bowl him over. He's there waiting for me." I knocked him over, and the ball and the glove and the mask and everything went. I was safe. I went in the dugout and a guy said, "Oh, you're going to get it. You better be loose when you get up there." I said, "What for?" He says, "What for? You knocked Danning over. You're going to get knocked down yourself. They're going to throw at you." I said, "Why? I couldn't get in." He said, "Well, you just be loose, that's all."

So I get up there, and the first pitch I'm thinking, "Well, maybe they'll throw at me," and sure enough, down I go. So the next pitch I say to myself, "Well, I'm not too sure they'll knock me down now." Boom! Down I go again. Now it's two and nothing. I'm thinking, "Well, he didn't hit me, but I don't know if he'll throw at me again," and wasn't quite as ready as the last time.

And he threw at me again, and down I went, and they said that the ball went between my cap and my head. My cap stayed up and the ball went right in between there. I'm down three and nothing. I think, "Well, now, I just don't think that he's going to walk me. He hasn't hit me, but I don't think he's going to walk me."

Well, the adrenaline's flowing by now, and he threw a ball high around the shoulders, and I came down on it, and I hit it over the roof at the Polo Grounds. The funny thing about it, when I went to Michigan State from Florida State to coach, the sportswriter Joe Falls mentioned that Danny Litwhiler was coming, and he said, "I'll never forget the day he was knocked down three times by Ace Adams. Then he got up the fourth time and hit one over top of the roof."

But they never threw at me after that.

A Hitting Bonus

In my rookie year, 1940, I came up in August, and had a 21-game hitting streak. It was stopped in the 22nd game. I hit a ground ball in the infield, and I thought I had it beat out, but the umpire called me out. Doc Prothro, the manager, got thrown out of the game because he was arguing with the call.

Right after that, Mr. Nugent, the president of the ballclub, called he in. He said, "I guess you know that the attendance went up because of your streak."

I said, "Well, I know we were getting more people."

He said, "We know why. It was because you were in this hitting streak. We'd like to give you a $500 bonus."

So I got a $500 bonus for a 21-game hitting streak. *[This was one year before Joe DiMaggio's record-setting 56 game hitting streak. Litwhiler played in 36 games and batted .345.]*

The Errorless Streak

[In 1942 with the Phillies, his second full season in the big leagues, outfielder Danny Litwhiler became the first player in the history of baseball to play a full season of 150 or more games without making an error. He was 26 years old at the end of the season. He describes a day when the streak was almost stopped.]

It was late in the season, and I'd played every game, every inning, and had no errors. It was in September in New York; we were playing the Giants in the Polo Grounds. We had a heavy downpour. The game was held up for about an hour and a half. They finally decided to play it. The infield was not in very good shape, and the outfield in left center was just a big pool of water, probably the size of the infield grass. About the seventh or eighth inning, Willard Marshall was on second base and Johnny Mize was the hitter. Mize hit a ball to left center, and I went to make the play. As I was coming in on the ball, I saw Willard Marshall take off for home. He figured it was a base hit, and I thought to myself, "I gotcha." So I went to make a shoestring catch, and just as I caught the ball and twisted to make the throw, I hit that water, and it just threw me and I slid maybe 35, 40 feet, with water just flying all over, and I dropped the ball. Well, I figured since it was a try at a shoestring catch anyway, it was probably a base hit. But as I went back to my position I saw the big E come down on the scoreboard, for Error. And I thought, "Oh, no, how could they give me an error on that? I go all year and get one on something like that, where you're going into the water and you slip and fall, or slide, and happen to drop the ball."

Almost as soon as the game's over, the papers are out around the subways and train stations. We were going back to Philadelphia that night, and I picked up a paper to see about having an error, the first one all year. And I had no error. There was nothing in the box score. I said, "I can't believe that. I saw the big E myself." The next morning, in Philadelphia, I got up about five-thirty or six o'clock to look at the paper, and there was no error listed in the box score. Nothing said about an error. I couldn't believe it. I went the complete season without making an error.

Ten years later I ran into Mel Allen at a banquet. He said, "Danny, you remember that day in the Polo Grounds where you slipped in the water and they gave you an error?"

I said, "Yeah, I do remember it. I found out later it was no error."

He said, "Let me tell you what happened."

Here's Mel's story: Johnny Mize, who hit the ball, was hitting .299, and he was trying to hit .300, which is a magic figure. When it was called an error, it took away a hit from him. As soon as the game was over, he went right up to the press box in his uniform and challenged the scorekeeper.

The scorekeeper said, "Well, I think it was an error."

Mize said, "How can you give him an error? The kid goes in, tries to make a shoestring catch and slides in the water. How can you give him an error, it's a clean base hit."

The scorekeeper said, "Well, it still looks like an error to me. What do you think, Mel?"

Mel said, "I think it was a hit."

Then the scorekeeper said, "Okay, it's a hit."

So I completed the complete season without making an error. *[Mize, a 29 year old, was in his seventh year in the league. He finished the season at .305. Mize batted over .300 in each of his first nine big league seasons. A Hall of Famer, Mize hit .312 lifetime with 359 home runs.]* Had Johnny Mize not been hitting .300 or close to it, I would have gotten an error, because he wouldn't have gone up to challenge the ruling.

The streak continued into 1943, and I'd gone 187 consecutive games without an error. A ball was hit in left center, and I went over to field it on the first hop. I got over there, and just as I was about to get in front of it, reaching out with my gloved hand, it hit something and it came back to my right side, and on the run I reached back with my right hand and tried to catch the ball and I never touched it. Earl Naylor, who was the center fielder, was right behind me, and he picked the ball up and the guy got a double on it. Well, they gave me a two-base error, and that was the only error I had the whole year. *[Litwhiler was traded from the Phillies to the pennant-winning Cardinals shortly after the errorless streak ended. In 1942-43 he had just that one error in 267 games, covering 533 putouts and 21 assists. Only twice in his 11-year career did he have more than three errors in a season.]*

Between Friends

The only time I had a problem with contracts was one time with the Phillies. Billy Cox bought the ballclub. He was from Brooklyn, and he had some race horses. When it came time for negotiating for a contract I went in and he was going to give me the same money. "Wait a minute," I said. "I think I deserve a raise." I was making $8,000 at the time. He said, "Well, I do, too. But I can't afford it right now. If the attendance is up substantially the first month, I'll give you a $2,000 raise." I said, "Well, that's fine, put it in the contract." He said, "No, no, no, we won't put it in the contract." I said, "What do you mean, you won't put it in the contract." He said, "Well, we don't have to have that in the contract. This is between friends. We'll shake hands on it." I said, "Well, I don't like it that way, but if you say that's the way to do it, I'll do it." He says, "Well, who knows how much money I win or lose on a horse race. I could win $2,000 easy on a horse race. No problem." So I said, "Okay." We started playing real good. Bucky Harris had the ballclub and we had a few good old ballplayers. Schoolboy Rowe came back; I think he won 16 for us that year. Anyway, the first month the attendance was way up in comparison to the other years. And he made a deal with St. Louis, and I was in that deal. I went to the Cardinals. They got three ballplayers from the Cardinals. Of course, I didn't see Cox at all. I was just told, "You're going to the Cardinals, pack up and go." So that's what I did. When I went over to the Cardinals I told them that I deserve a $2,000 raise. I explained it to him, and Sam Breadon said, "Well, if you deserve the $2,000, you get it out of Billy Cox, I didn't agree to that." So I lost out on the $2,000.

'44 World Series

Hitting a home run in the 1944 World Series, in the fifth game off Nelson Potter, was a big moment. We were tied with the Browns two games to two, and we were leading 1-0 in the eighth. I hit a home run and we won 2-0, and that was quite a thrill. *[The Cardinals won the Series in six games.]*

I happened to hit it in right field, right center, and normally I never hit long balls to right field. I pulled everything. When I hit the ball out there, I just thought, "Oh, gosh, a fly ball." I'm rounding first base, and I heard the crowd really screaming. We were playing in Sportsman's Park, which is the Browns' and the Cardinals' home field, and I didn't know who was screaming and cheering, and I thought, "Yeah, that stupid Brownie out there made a great catch probably," and I looked out and saw the ball bouncing around the grandstand. I hit a home run there, and I just couldn't believe I hit one.

I don't know if I touched the bases or not.

Potter was a good competitor, he had a good screwball. That's what he threw me. He got it high, and that's where I hit it, to right field, or right center, I believe it was. But he was a good pitcher, nobody wore him out too much.

Enos Slaughter

I saw Enos Slaughter pop a ball up, I mean high, one of those major league popups, and he takes off—he always did. See, that's the difference between the ballplayers today and the ballplayers when I played. If you popped up and didn't run that ball out to first base, you were fined.

Well, he put his head down and took off. That ball was played as a fair ball. It was kind of misplayed in the infield because it was high or the sun or some reason. It kind of rolled away a little bit and Enos slid into third base. He got a three-base error on a pop fly in the infield.

Batting Practice Pays

In 1938 I ended up in Alexandria, Louisiana, Class D. I got down there and the manager said, "Well, what'd they send you here for?"

I said, "I guess to play ball, I don't know."

He said, "I can only pay you a $100 a month."

I said, "Well, I want a hundred and a quarter."

He said, "Take some batting practice." Well, they had a batboy who threw nice batting practice. They had a fairly short fence, and I started popping the ball over the fence.

He said, "That's it. Okay. Come in, I'll sign you up."

So I got a hundred and a quarter.

Bobby Malkmus

Six years (1957-62)
Born July 4, 1931 BR TR 5'9" 175 lbs.
Positions: 2B, 114; SS, 65; 3B, 39
Milwaukee Braves, Washington Senators, Philadelphia Phillies

G	BA	AB	H	2B	3B	HR	R	RBI	BB	SO	SB	FA
268	.215	572	123	15	5	8	69	46	38	90	3	.978

*M*alkmus played 121 games for the Phillies in 1961 as backup to Tony Taylor at second, Ruben Amaro at short, and Charlie Smith at third. He hit .231, his career high, and hit seven of his eight career home runs. He played 11 years in the minors, four times hitting better than .290 for full seasons. In 1956 he led the Texas League with 11 triples and 21 stolen bases. In 1959 he hit .300 with 16 home runs for Denver in the American Association. He became a minor league manager after his playing career ended in the Pacific Coast League in 1966.

Lesson from Campanella

I guess it was my sixth game in the major leagues. We were playing the Dodgers, and I wasn't in the line-up. Drysdale is pitching and we're hitting him pretty good. Johnny Logan was kind of a popoffish guy, and he's popping off on the bench to Drysdale, and Drysdale looked over into the dugout, and knowing Johnny Logan, you could tell his voice anywhere.

So the next inning we were hitting and he gets his bat and goes up into the on deck circle and as he's on the way out of the dugout, he says, "Fellas, get ready."

When he got up to the plate, the first pitch was in his ribs. He started walking to first, and all of a sudden he ran for the pitcher's mound, and both teams then ran out onto the field. Del Crandall was my roomie, so I hung close to him. We're walking back, and he's walking next to Campanella, along with me, and Campanella's got all his garb on, his mask, chest protector, shin guards and so forth.

Del says to him, "How come in the fight you keep your mask on?"

He says, "Well, when I first came up to the big leagues, I was a rookie, I took my mask off and I got a mouth full of knuckles." He says, "No more."

The Bald Facts

When I first got to the big leagues in Milwaukee nobody knew me as being a bald-headed guy. I always changed my hat to my helmet real quick.

We were playing the Cardinals in a night game. Murry Dickson threw a knuckleball and it danced at me and it was heading for my head and I just bailed out. In bailing out I knocked off my helmet, and there I'm lying on the ground feeling for my helmet to put it on quick and I can hear the people—there's some 40,000 people in the stands—snickering, you know.

So I get back up at the plate and getting ready to hit again, and Hal Smith, the catcher, says, "Bob, for a rookie, you're balder than I am."

I don't know if it was funny or embarrassing. Since then I haven't worried too much about letting people know I'm bald.

Spahn's No-Hitter

We *[the Phillies]* were playing the Braves and Warren Spahn in Milwaukee. Spahnnie, as we all called him, was pitching a no-hitter. With two outs in the ninth inning I came to the plate. I hit a line drive back at Spahnnie. He got his glove up in time to deflect the ball behind the rubber. Johnny Logan came charging in and picked the ball up barehanded and threw on the run to first base. The throw was in the dirt at first and Joe Adcock scooped up the throw. The umpire called me out at first to end the game, and Spahnnie had his no-hitter. *[September 15, 1960—4-0, the first of Spahn's two no-hitters. The second was a 1-0 win over the San Francisco Giants on April 28, 1961, at Milwaukee.]*

Frank Malzone

Twelve years (1955-66)
Born Feb. 28, 1930 BR TR 5'10" 180 lbs.
Position: Third Base
Boston Red Sox, California Angels

G	BA	AB	H	2B	3B	HR	R	RBI	BB	SO	SB	FA
1441	.274	5428	1486	239	21	133	647	728	337	434	14	.955

Malzone was a five-time All-Star and a three-time Gold Glove winner, including the first Gold Glove awarded, in 1957, when they gave only nine awards for the two leagues. In his first full season, 1957, he drove in 103 runs and hit 15 home runs. That year he became the first player in modern baseball history to lead his position in games played, putouts, assists, errors, double plays, and fielding percentage. From 1957-64 Frank averaged almost 153 games a season and never hit fewer than 13 home runs in any season. He played eight minor league seasons, and missed two seasons (1952-53) for military service. In 1949 he led the Canadian-American League with 26 triples while batting .329. He hit .310 with 88 RBIs for Louisville of the American Association in 1955.

Rookie of the Year Controversy

I was considered a rookie almost all the way through the 1957 season. You know, the writers would write 'rookie' and all that. All of a sudden it got down to the last month of the season and the New York writers decided to take a vote on whether Frank Malzone is a rookie or not, because I was up a month and a half the year before. *[In 1956 Malzone played 27 games with 103 at-bats and a .165 average]*

The New York writers voted that I wasn't a rookie. They wanted to get the New York player as Rookie of the Year and Tony Kubek won it. I think Dan Daniels was the head of the writers at that time. It probably cost me some money, not being Rookie of the Year. *[That year Malzone hit .292 in 153 games with 15 home runs and 103 RBIs; Kubek hit .297 in 127 games with three home runs and 39 RBIs. Malzone also won the Gold Glove that year, the first year it was given, as the best fielding third baseman in the major leagues. The next year they gave separate awards for American and National League.]*

As I got to know Tony, I didn't feel too bad because he's a great guy. But at the time I was a little disappointed, realizing what it means both for the money and with the name recognition. I just didn't think the New York writers had the right to make a judgment on something like that.

Playing to Win

I was on eight All-Star teams and played in seven games *[Malzone was on All-Star teams in five separate years; they had two games some years]*. A special moment has to be the one in Baltimore *[in 1958]*. We were tied in the sixth inning. I got a single to lead off

Frank Malzone

the inning and scored the winning run. Another All-Star thrill was hitting a home run off Don Drysdale in the 1959 game.

My first All-Star game was in 1957. Ted Williams and I were the two Red Sox players named to the team. I remember talking to Ted on the plane going to St. Louis. He told me how important the All-Star game was to the American League. By the time I got there I realized it was important to the American League to win the game for the prestige of it; it wasn't just an exhibition type of atmosphere.

I was the alternate third baseman. George Kell was selected by the fans. I picked him up after the fourth inning. Casey Stengel was the manager. We ended up winning the ballgame. *[AL won 6-5; each team scored three runs in the ninth.]*

It was quite a thrill to be a winner the first year you play on an All-Star team. I wasn't considered a youngster; I was 27 years old— but still, being there and playing with Mantle, Ted Williams, Al Kaline and all the great players who were in the American League and playing against all the great National League players. You know, even though you do it a number of times, you still approach it with nervousness until the day arrives, until you go through the ballgame.

It was always quite a thrill, and you don't think about those things until later on in your career and later on in life when you sit back and you realize what a great accomplishment it really was. You know, you don't really realize it at the time.

Marty Marion

Thirteen years (1940-50, 52-53)
Born Dec. 1, 1917   BR   TR   6'2"   170 lbs.
Position: Shortstop, 3B, 2
St. Louis Cardinals, St. Louis Browns

G	BA	AB	H	2B	3B	HR	R	RBI	BB	SO	SB	FA
1572	.263	5506	1448	272	37	36	602	624	470	537	35	.969

A seven-time All-Star, Marion was the NL MVP in 1944. He played on four pennant-winning and three World Championship Cardinal teams. Considered the best defensive shortstop of his day, he averaged 140 games during his first nine seasons in spite of a bad back that plagued him throughout much of his career. A consistent hitter, he batted between .272 and .280 in six of his first nine seasons. He managed the Cardinals, Browns, and White Sox.

It's Easier to Win with Talent

There's not much to tell about when I managed the Browns, except we lost every day. *[Marion's record with the club in 1952 was 42-61. In 1953 it was 54-100. In two full seasons as White Sox manager in 1955 and 1956, he led them to two third place finishes, going 91-63 and 85-69.]* Other than that, it was a pretty miserable year. But unfortunately, if you don't have talent, you can't win. Hornsby was fired because he wasn't winning. If they were winning, Hornsby would still be here. Marion would still be here if they were winning. It's the easiest thing in the world to fire the manager because of fan's assumptions. You can't fire all the players.

I loved managing. I tried to outfigure everybody, I tried to outsmart everybody, all that kind of stuff. But one thing I did not like about managing: you cannot control the destiny of what the other people do. It's up to the players to make you a manager or not make you a manager. You can't make them play better. If they have the ability and they play up to their ability, that's all you can ask. Some people are just better than others. The successful managers are people who have talent on their ballclub. Give me the players, I'll be a great manager.

The Old Rock Pile

All the visiting teams hated to come to St. Louis because we had a ballpark that the Browns and the Cardinals both played on, and it was in pretty bad shape. We called it The Old Rock Pile. If you could play there, you could play anywhere.

By about June we didn't have any grass on the field. It was all worn out. It was all natural grass, and because two teams played on it, it never rested. But it was a good place to play for the St. Louis Cardinals, and pretty tough for the guys who came in there because we were used to the field and the heat.

I used to love to play in Crosley Field. When you're an in-fielder, the only thing you look at is, "How good is the infield?" Are there bad hops? Crosley Field was great. I never did like to play in a ballpark that had too hard an infield, except St. Louis; I knew where all the bounces were. I liked to play on a soft infield. But I didn't have the luxury of ever playing on Astroturf; I only played on grass, and most of the time the ballparks back in those days weren't kept like they are now. Now, they have a crew that probably makes millions of dollars just to keep the grass green. But we didn't have that luxury.

Cal McLish

Fifteen years (1944, 46-49, 51, 56-64)
Born Dec. 1, 1925 BB TR 6'0" 179 lbs.
Position: Pitcher
Brooklyn Dodgers, Pittsburgh Pirates, Chicago Cubs, Cleveland
Indians, Cincinnati Reds, Chicago White Sox, Philadelphia Phillies

G	W	L	PCT	ERA	GS	CG	SV	IP	H	BB	SO	BA	FA
352	92	92	.500	4.01	207	57	6	1609	1684	552	713	.149	.975

McLish was an All-Star in 1959, when he won 19 and lost eight for Cleveland, after posting a 16-8 record for the Indians in 1958. After the 1959 season he was traded with Billy Martin and Gordy Coleman to the Reds for Johnny Temple. In 1960 he was traded with Juan Pizzaro to the White Sox. In 1961 he was traded to the Phillies with Frank Barnes and Andy Carey. Without ever playing in the minor leagues, he pitched with the Dodgers in 1944 as an 18-year-old, then spent two years in the military in Europe. Between 1947-55 he won 102 minor league games, mostly with Los Angeles of the Pacific Coast League. He hit three big league home runs, two of them in 1957 with Cleveland. His given name is perhaps baseball's longest: Calvin Coolidge Julius Caesar Tuskahoma McLish.

Trying to Be a Nice Guy

I got called into the clubhouse on Friday of the last week of the season in 1959. I was supposed to start the last game of the season on Sunday, and I would have had a chance to win 20 ballgames. Joe Gordon, the manager, was there, and the pitching coach Mel Harder, and Frank Lane, the general manager. They told me, "We'd like for you to give up your start Sunday so we can pitch Herb Score, so he can pitch without pressure." Naturally, I readily agreed, you know, because I knew I wasn't going to set any records for 20-win seasons.

I thought I was being a professional about it, not knowing that I had been traded to the Cincinnati Reds. The deal hadn't been announced yet, but about two weeks after I got home, a sportswriter, Hal Liebowitz, called me and said, "You've been traded." I wouldn't have thought a heck of a lot about it or it wouldn't have mattered quite as much if I'd been traded in the American League. The first thought went through my mind, maybe the Yankees. He said, "You've been traded to Cincinnati."

So now I'm going back to the league where I started, where I got off to a bad start at Brooklyn, 3 and 10, and then 4 and 10 in Chicago—that's 7 and 20, you know. I didn't want to leave the American League because I'd learned the hitters in the American League and with my style of pitching, I had to know the hitters. So I was disappointed, to say the least, that I got traded out of the league.

Cleveland had a bunch of good young arms—Gary Bell, Mudcat Grant, Jim Perry, Hank Aguirre—so I could see why they would trade me, but the fact that I was 16-8 the year before and then 19-8 in 1959, and I was kind of the leader of the staff, you might say, and I really enjoyed the fact that I was in a solid rotation with a bunch of young, good-looking pitchers, and it was something to look forward to. Then when I got the news that I'd been traded it was very disappointing, especially knowing that I'd given up my chance to win 20, thinking I was being a nice guy. Well, now I wish I hadn't a been a nice guy.

Called Before Judge Landis

In 1943, a year before I signed with the Dodgers, I'd gone as a guest of the Cardinals to watch a doubleheader, the Cubs against the Cardinals, and in that trip I was taken in front of Judge Landis *[baseball commissioner]* at the Chase Hotel.

Me and LeRoy Jarvis, a catcher, had signed an agreement on a napkin to work out with the Washington Senators, with all our expenses paid. And they tried to make a contract out of it. When I was called up in front of Judge Landis he asked me about that. That was a kind of a scary thing, because he was kind of a grumpy old guy. And from that came the rule that no club could sign a high school kid until he or his class graduated.

The Hanging Curve

Cal McLish pitched in the big leagues for fifteen years and was a 19-game winner for Cleveland in 1959. He offers, in verse, these pitching tips:

The Hanging Curve

Year after year I've heard them say,
"It's the base on balls that turns managers grey."

The thought that grates most on the manager's nerves
Is the dreaded fear of those hanging curves.

It's the one pitch that surely will seal your fate
If you hang it up high out over the plate.

The next pitch to it is the slider that's flat;
Hitters don't miss it 'cause it speeds up the bat.

So if you throw these, get a good tight spin
Or stay with the speed low away or high in.

And upset his timing, use a good change of pace.
Make the manager happy; keep your team in the race.

Develop good rhythm; be mechanically sound;
Keep the ball in the park, get your outs on the ground.

Hold all runners close, don't give them a jump.
Keep the batter off base; help him stay in his slump.

If you don't want sure victories snatched by defeats,
Don't let three run homers land out in the seats.

Be careful about what kind of pitch has been called;
That hanging curve will make managers bald.

Pete Milne

Three years (1948-50)
Born Apr. 10, 1925 BL TR 6'1" 180 lbs.
Position: Outfield
New York Giants

G	BA	AB	H	2B	3B	HR	R	RBI	BB	SO	SB	FA
47	.233	60	14	1	2	1	6	9	4	13	0	.882

A speedy outfielder, Milne was used mostly as a pinch-hitter for the Giants, going 7-29. He played in the field in only 10 of his 47 big league games. His only big league home run was a pinch hit, inside-the-park grand slam. In his big league debut he went 3-4 against Warren Spahn. He played pro ball for 14 years, several of them in the Pacific Coast League, finishing second one year in hitting behind Bob Dillinger.

Examining Musial's Bat

We went to St. Louis and I was sitting beside Walker Cooper while the Cardinals were taking batting practice. Cooper had caught for St. Louis for years. When Musial threw his bat down, Walker said, "Go out there and get that bat, Pete." He said it would be all right because he knew Musial real well, played with him for years. So I went out there and got the bat.

When I looked at it, I knew why he wanted me to look at it. On most bats you'll see where guys have hit it up near the trademark, you know. Little scruff marks. On that bat, the hitting surface where you're supposed to hit the ball was just about flat. He didn't have any marks on the rest of the bat. He hit the ball in the same place on the bat just about all the time.

He was a good line drive hitter. Now I saw Ted Williams hit, too, and he was a great hitter, a great hitter. He was just an overpowering hitter. But Musial could hit line drives right down the left field line. Ted could have, if he had wanted to. But he wouldn't do it. They all shifted around on him, he was just going to show them he could still hit the ball in there. But Musial, you pitch him outside, I mean make a great pitch on him, and he'll beat you. That helped me, by observing and seeing things like that.

Knocking Musial Down

In '49, Musial started the season kind of slow. He hadn't been doing much at all when he came into Brooklyn. They were going to play Brooklyn and they were on to the Polo Grounds to play us. Well, he caught fire in Brooklyn. Man, he was hitting. He hit a ton over there. He was hitting them out of the ballpark and against the walls and everything.

We had a left handed pitcher, Monte Kennedy, that could throw the ball through a brick wall, but he had wild streaks. In fact,

I saw him one day out in Cincinnati for nine innings throw fast balls by the Cincinnati ballclub, and they had Ted Kluszewski and guys like that on it.

But anyhow, they came in there, and Monte was pitching, and Durocher told him, "You knock him down when he comes up. You've got to cool him off."

And I mean Monte decked him. There wasn't no question about it, the pitchers would knock anybody down, try to protect themselves. A guy got hot, you know. So Monte drilled one in there and unwound him.

Musial gets up and dusts himself off. And he hits a shot right into the right field bleachers.

The second time up, Durocher said, "Knock him down twice." And he did. He floored him twice.

Now Musial didn't get up and glare and raise hell and cuss everybody out like some players do when they get thrown at. He just got up and he dusted himself off and he just chewed that gum a little faster, and he wound himself up, and the next one he hit it into the second deck in right center, like a shot.

The third time he come up Monte said, "What do you want me to do, Skip?"

Durocher said, "Walk him."

That's what you call a great hitter.

Pinch Hit, Inside-the-Park Grand Slam

On April 27, 1949 we played Brooklyn. We led 6-0, then the Dodgers came back to take an 8-6 lead. In the seventh, we filled the bases with a couple of walks and an infield single, and Leo Durocher said to me, "Grab a bat and go up and hit for Hansen."

My heart began pumping. I can still see the first pitch coming in. It was a fast ball, just below waist high over the outside part of the plate. I lashed at it and hit it good. I got every bit of it. The Polo Grounds is a football field, so it was almost 500 feet to centerfield. I hit a shot of a line drive and Duke Snider went after it but couldn't get to it. He chased it to the wall and by the time the ball got back to the infield I had rounded the bases.

The *New York Daily News* had a huge picture of me sliding and Roy Campanella still waiting for the throw. The headline read: "Milne's four-run homer beats Bums." When I left the stadium people were everywhere. Of course, I didn't mind it. It was the first time they'd paid attention to me. I got telegrams from all over the country from everybody I knew.

The next day I was sitting on the bench again, waiting for another chance to pinch hit. It was my only major league homer, and a writer from *Baseball Digest* has researched the hit and believes it is the only pinch hit, inside-the-park grand slam in history.

Almost a Cub

I loved to play in Chicago. The fans were right down on top of you. And they were great fans. If you made a good play they'd give you a big hand, just like they did their own people. I almost had a chance to play there in '49. Frankie Frisch was a coach for the Giants when the season opened, and after about six weeks of the season, the Cubs fired their manager, Charlie Grimm. Frankie Frisch went over there as manager. Before it was even announced, he came to my hotel room in New York and told me, "Pete, I'm going to manage the Cubs. I need a center fielder. You go out to the ballpark and get all the hitting you can, all the batting practice you can, and keep your bag packed because I've already talked to Mr. Wrigley and he said if there's any way possible, you're going to get a chance to play every day."

Boy, I was in hog heaven, let me tell you. I was out at the ballpark before the damn equipment boys got out there. I was there at eight-thirty waiting for them to open it up. I was getting extra batting practice, working out.

Right after that we left on our Western swing. I kept waiting to hear from them, and we went into Chicago, there was a note in my box to call Frankie Frisch and had his telephone number. And boy, my heart got to beating, and I thought, "Great, I'm going to get to play against the Giants today." 'Cause I could see I wasn't going to play on the Giants. They were set. All three guys that year had a great year.

Willard Marshall had a terrible spring training, and I had a great spring training. Hell, I hit close to four hundred in the spring. I tore the ball up, and I really won the damn job. But Durocher told me, "I'm going to start Marshall because we're trying to make a deal." But he started off at the beginning of the season and hit great. In fact, all three of those guys were hitting .330 or above, all the first part of the season. So I couldn't even get in the line-up. *[For the season Marshall, in right, hit .307; Thomson, in center, hit .309; Lockman, in left, hit .301.]* So anyway, I called Frisch and he told me, "Pete, we tried everything. Mr. Wrigley told Horace Stoneham, 'Just write down what you want, we need a center fielder.' And he wouldn't do it." And there wasn't one damn thing I could do about it.

Bobby Morgan

Eight years (1950, 52-58)

Born June 29, 1926 BR TR 5'9" 175 lbs.

Positions: 2B, 232; SS, 211; 3B, 190; 1B, 1

Brooklyn Dodgers, Philadelphia Phillies,

St. Louis Cardinals, Chicago Cubs

G	BA	AB	H	2B	3B	HR	R	RBI	BB	SO	SB	FA
671	.233	2088	487	96	11	53	286	217	327	381	18	.963

*M*organ was backup third baseman for the Dodgers behind Billy Cox in 1950, 1952, and 1953. He appeared in the 1952 and 1953 World Series with the Dodgers. He was traded to the Phillies in 1954 and was their regular shortstop in 1954 and their starting second baseman in 1955, playing in over 130 games each year. In May, 1956 he was traded to the Cardinals for Solly Hemus. Six months later he was traded back to the Phillies with Rip Repulski for Del Ennis. Morgan played five full minor league seasons. With Spokane in 1947 he had a league-leading 18 triples. In 1949 with Montreal he was the International League's MVP with a league-leading .337 average, a league-leading 38 doubles. He also hit 19 home runs and drove in 112 runs.*

A Great Country

My first big-league game was in Philadelphia, the opening game of the season, 1950, and I was playing third base. This was my first big-league game with the Dodgers. They played the National Anthem, I looked around—Shotgun Shuba's in left and Duke Snider's in center and Jackie Robinson is playing second. Gil Hodges is at first, and Carl Furillo is playing right field, and I think Carl Erskine was pitching and Campanella was catching. I looked around and said, "My gosh, can you believe this? Is this a great country or what?"

And at shortstop, just a few feet to my left, my childhood idol, Pee Wee Reese. As a boy in Oklahoma City, I'd dreamed my whole life of being a ballplayer. Just being on the same field, in the same line-up, was as great an honor as I could ever want. I looked at his black No. 1 on his back and I said, "Good gracious, what a lucky guy I am."

Signing

There were three of us here in Oklahoma City that played Little League ball together and American Legion ball together. The other two were Cal McLish, who pitched in the big leagues for a long time *[McLish pitched 15 years in the big leagues; he won 92 and lost 92]*, and LeRoy Jarvis, who was a catcher for Pittsburgh *[Jarvis played 21 games for Pittsburgh between 1944-47]*.

We were all childhood buddies, and a scout by the name of Tom Greenwade came into town. He'd signed a lot of ballplayers for the Dodgers and the Yankees. Tom wanted to sign all three of us, and my mom wanted me to finish school. So he signed Calvin and LeRoy in 1944, the spring, and they went to Bear Mountain, New York, for spring training with the Dodgers. I finished school, and Tom Greenwade came back after about a month before school ended. He signed me, and that made a threesome that he signed right out of Oklahoma City at one time, and all three of us played in the big leagues. So it was quite a deal. We were all very thrilled about it.

Red Murff

Two years (1956-57)

Born April 1, 1921 BR TR 6'3" 195 lbs.

Position: Pitcher

Milwaukee Braves

G	W	L	PCT	ERA	GS	CG	SV	IP	H	BB	SO	BA	FA
26	2	2	.500	4.65	2	0	3	50.1	56	18	31	.091	.941

The scout who signed Nolan Ryan, Red Murff was a long time minor league pitching star. He won 27 games with a league-leading 1.99 ERA for Dallas (Double A Texas League) in 1955, earning him Minor League Player of the Year honors. He was brought up to the majors by the Braves in 1956 at the age of 35 but an arm injury ended his career. After his playing career ended, he scouted for the Houston Colt 45's, New York Mets, Montreal Expos, Atlanta Braves and Chicago, signing dozens of other major league players, including Jerry Koosman, Jerry Grote, and Mike Stanton. Red was inducted into the Texas Baseball Hall of Fame in 1989.

Spahn's Theory

Spahn's theory of winning 20 ballgames was: "You're going to get 35 starts, and five of them will not be decisions. So you've got 30 decisions. If you're 15-15, you're a good pitcher. You can make it 16-14 if you're a good hitter. You can make it 17-13 if you're a good fielder. You can make it 18-12 if you're a good runner. And you can scramble like hell to get those other two." And that was his theory. *[Spahn started between 32 and 39 games for 17 straight seasons.]* Those other two you can get if you will just pull a little bit harder.

So I thought his theory was excellent, you're a .500 pitcher if you throw strikes with major league equipment. But he had it figured out, and it's easy to see that he was successful. He played a lot of years and set a lot of records. I enjoyed my association with those big people like Spahn. He probably would have chosen to be an outfielder today, with the DH, because he was that kind of hitter. If he's taking batting practice and getting acquainted with pitchers every day, he could have been a three hundred hitter in the major leagues, I'm sure, and he would have hit a lot of home runs.

Williams, on the Mechanics of Pitching

Just get the mechanics right, and pitching is a simple process. I learned that from Ted Williams. "How can you tell what a pitch is going to be, Ted?" And at the time we were talking, there were about three black pitchers in the league.

He said, "Well, as soon as you see the white part of a pitcher's wrist. That's the inside of it, just where the palm breaks and back in there where it's protected from the sun nearly all the time. That is the part that indicates to me that he's coming at me with a fast ball or a straight change. When I see that, at the moment he raises that arm behind his head to project the ball, I know it's a fast ball from that time on, and I gear for a fast ball. If he changes up on me, I can still hit the ball the other way. When I don't see that, I know it's a curve ball."

That's the mechanics of pitching that he taught me.

Bob Oldis

Seven years (1953-55, 60-63)
Born Jan. 5, 1928 BR TR 6'1" 185 lbs.
Positions: Catcher, 3B, 2
Washington Senators, Pittsburgh Pirates, Philadelphia Phillies

G	BA	AB	H	2B	3B	HR	R	RBI	BB	SO	SB	FA
135	.237	236	56	6	0	1	20	22	20	22	0	.983

*O*ldis appeared in two games in the 1960 World Series for the Pirates. In his final season, 1963, he saw his most action, appearing in 47 games and batting 85 times for the Phillies as backup to Clay Dalrymple. He spent four full seasons in the minors before his first big-league appearance, batting between .277 and .289 each year.

Bad Timing

The only home run I hit was in Dodger Stadium *[in 1962, playing with the Phillies]*. I came back and everybody was quiet in the dugout. I was more surprised than anybody. But they had towels laid out all the way in the dugout for me and everything else. And real quiet.

And then they all busted up laughing like hell. It put us ahead, but then we blew it in about the seventh or eighth inning. We got beat.

It was on a Saturday night, so the people in the Midwest never did see that I hit a home run, because it was a Saturday night game in L.A. and never made the Midwest papers on Sunday.

And on Monday they were talking about the Sunday afternoon games.

I hit it off of Pete Richert. I send him a Christmas card every year and thank him.

The Right Place at the Right Time

I was with the Yankee organization in 1959 and the Pirates called me after I got home that year. They said, "We're thinking about drafting you in the winter draft for $25,000 if you'd like to go play ball in the Dominican," and I said, "Darn right."

So we went to the Dominican, and then in the first week of December, the Pirates drafted me for $25,000. I was at the right place at the right time.

As you know, I didn't play much. I was a hell of a cheerleader, though. I think I played what, 22 games that year *[caught in 22 games, batted four for 20]*, but it was being at the right place at the right time with a bunch of winning players. They knew how to win, and beat the Yankees in the World Series, and I got to play two games in the World Series. *[Oldis caught in two games, did not bat.]*

Milt Pappas

Seventeen years (1957-73)
Born May 11, 1939 BR TR 6'3" 190 lbs.
Position: Pitcher
Baltimore Orioles, Cincinnati Reds,
Atlanta Braves, Chicago Cubs

G	W	L	PCT	ERA	GS	CG	SV	IP	H	BB	SO	BA	FA
520	209	164	.560	3.40	465	129	4	3185.2	3046	858	1728	.123	.969

*B*orn Miltiades Stergios Papastegios, Milt is 36th on the
All-Time list with 43 shutouts, more than Hall of Famers
Sandy Koufax and Catfish Hunter, only two fewer than Whitey
Ford, Robin Roberts, and Phil Niekro, and just three behind Bob
Feller and Tommy John. Milt pitched just three minor league games
before coming to the big leagues at age 18. He won in double figures
in his first 11 full seasons. He had only three losing seasons in 17
years. In 1959 at the age of 20 he went 15-9 with Baltimore, completing 15 of his 27 starts. In 1972 he went 17-7 with the Cubs
with a 2.77 ERA and a no-hitter, the only base-runner being Larry
Stahl on a two-out walk in the ninth inning. A two-time All-Star
(1962, 65) he was only one NL win away from winning 100 games

in each league. A dangerous hitter, 20 of his 132 hits were home runs, including two in one game in 1961. Baltimore traded him to the Reds with Jack Balschun and Dick Simpson in 1965 for Frank Robinson, and Robinson won the Triple Crown with the Orioles in 1966.

The Spoiler

Back in the early sixties, the Minnesota Twins had a heck of a ball team. They had Tony Oliva, Earl Battey, Bob Allison, and Killebrew and so on, and I was pitching against them in Minneapolis. I had a no-hitter going into the eighth inning and got the first guy out. The second guy up was Zoilo Versailles, and we're winning five or six to nothing, and I said, well, there's no way this guy, especially being behind this many runs, will be swinging at the first pitch. So I threw a fast ball and he swung at it and he got a base hit. So I ended up with a one-hitter. I should have been more careful with him.

A Thrill

It was quite an honor to be selected to appear in the All-Star game. I started the one in 1965. The fact of getting to meet some of the guys you pitch against and play against but you never really get to meet was a nice situation, and I was really thrilled by it.

Before the game, it was all buddy-buddy, but once the game started and the adrenaline flowed you tried to beat the hell out of them. Obviously you didn't want to be the team that lost, especially when you had the greatest stars in the world playing that one particular day. *[Pappas was the starting pitcher for the American League but got no decision in the National League's 6-5 win.]*

Herb Plews

Four years (1956-59)

Born June 14, 1928   BL   TR   5'11"   160 lbs.

Positions: 2B, 217; 3B, 49; SS, 9

Washington Senators, Boston Red Sox

G	BA	AB	H	2B	3B	HR	R	RBI	BB	SO	SB	FA
346	.262	1017	266	42	17	4	125	82	74	133	3	.959

*P*lews hit .270 in 91 games in his rookie season, 1956, with the Senators. He followed that with .271 in 104 games his next season. On September 26, 1958 he participated in five double plays at second base, tying a since-broken major league record. In February, 1956, he was traded from the Yankee system with Lou Berberet, Bob Wiesler, and Dick Tettelbach for Mickey McDermott and Bobby Kline. He was traded to the Red Sox in 1959 for Billy Consolo. In the minors, he hit .304 for Norfork of the Piedmont League in 1953. The next year he hit .299 for Birmingham of the Southern Association and led the league with 16 triples. In 1955 he hit .302 for Denver, the Yankees' Triple A team, in the American Association.

The Washington Senators

You never knew what was going to happen with our club, because every night was a new situation. We always finished last; you know that, how it was with Washington, but at the time we had a fine group of fellows, and we all got along good. Nobody was making any extra money. We were always in about the same boat, so we did get along good, and we had some more or less characters on the team, Clint Courtney and Rocky Bridges and some of those fellows.

Rocky had most of his career with Cincinnati, I believe. He might have been with the Dodgers for awhile, but he reminded me of Don Zimmer. He was a similar-type player, more or less. Built stocky and he had a million stories to tell. And he just kind of kept you laughing all the time. If it wasn't just the way he looked at you it was saying something that was comical or humorous. He was just fun to be around.

Eddie Yost not only was a fine ballplayer, but just a real personable fellow. You couldn't help but like Eddie. He was just even-keeled all the way. It didn't matter if you won or lost from day to day, Eddie was just the same, and he went out there and gave you a hundred percent every day. Before I got to Washington, I didn't have any idea about him. I knew he walked; that was his mainstay, being able to walk a lot. And I thought he was probably a small statured man, not too tall or anything. When I saw him I was really surprised, because he was a well-built man. Well, he must have been six feet tall and probably a 195 pounds. I couldn't believe he was a leadoff hitter. He looked more like a third or fourth hitter. *[Yost was 5-10 and 170 pounds. He led the league in walks six times, and is seventh on the all-time list for number of walks. He hit .254 with 139 homers in his 18-year big-league career.]*

Herb Plews

A Bunch of Good Fellows

The umpires were great. I remember my first year up there. Different umpires would tell me, being an infielder, "Now be careful with so-and-so on first, he likes to slide hard," or something like that. I found the umps real good that way. They helped me out. I never argued with them, that was a waste of time anyhow. I got along good with them. They were a good bunch of fellows.

J.W. Porter

Six years (1952, 55-59)

Born Jan. 17, 1933 BR TR 6'2" 180 lbs.

Positions: Catcher, 91; OF, 62; 1B, 16; 3B, 3

St. Louis Browns, Detroit Tigers, Cleveland Indians,

Washington Senators, St. Louis Cardinals

G	BA	AB	H	2B	3B	HR	R	RBI	BB	SO	SB	FA
229	.228	544	124	22	1	8	58	62	53	96	4	.983

J.W. (his given name) came up to the big leagues at age 19 and hit .250 that year in 33 games, mostly as an outfielder. In 1951, at age 18, he caught 117 games for Waterloo in the Three-I League and batted .302 with 15 home runs, seven triples, and 95 RBIs. In 1952 he hit .340 in 66 games for Colorado Springs in the Western League. He was the American Legion Player of the Year in 1950. Porter is in the American Legion Hall of Fame at Cooperstown.

Touring Mantle's Home Runs

In 1956, when Mantle had his great Triple Crown year, he actually made our ballpark in Detroit look like a Little League park. I think he hit 11 home runs in Detroit, and each one farther than the one before. When somebody would join your ballclub in July, maybe a new pitcher or some guy you knew from the minor leagues, and you went down to the bullpen with them, you'd say, "You see that row? Mantle hit one off of Foytack. And you see up there in deep right center? Count the rows, two from the top and three over from there. He hit one off of Bunning up there."

He actually hit a ball into dead center field—and this is hard to believe, but ask Bob Miller about it—Mantle hit a line drive off Miller, a lefthander. Miller thinks it ticked an ear. The ball went in the upper deck in Detroit. Four hundred and forty feet to the base of the fence. Now we're talking 440 plus the height. Miller walked to the back of the mound, threw up, and walked off the field, met the manager halfway who was coming to get him anyway. But the manager didn't need to bother coming out 'cause Miller was gone. He wasn't pitching any more that day. You see golf balls do things like that, but you don't see many baseballs do that.

But the man was just the strongest, for his size, the fastest, who ever played. He'd strike out three or four times in a row, but then he'd beat out a bunt and the next time up would hit one downtown. You know, that's a baseball expression, meaning a home run. Well, when Mantle hit one downtown, it went downtown.

Musial and JFK

Musial was a fabulous, fabulous guy. I got to play and sit right next to Musial for a couple months, and it was a wonderful, wonderful experience. In fact, I was with him the day he met John F. Kennedy in the story that's told all over the country. We were standing in front of the hotel in Milwaukee. We had taken a walk, and we had were coming back to the hotel all these black limousines are pulling up. People are congregating. We don't know why. So we get up near the doors, as close to the doors to our hotel as we can. Then we realize that, as young Kennedy gets out—this was before the election, he was out looking for votes. So as he's walking into the front door of the hotel with the Secret Service, he looks over and he recognizes Musial. He pushes his way right through the crowd and he comes over and sticks out his hand and says, "Mr. Musial, I'm John Kennedy." Stan says, "Of course." Stan was a good Catholic boy himself. "I know exactly who you are." And he introduced me to him. So then Kennedy made the quote that's been quoted many times since. He said, "In both our cases let's prove them wrong. Let's prove to them that you're not too old to play ball and that I'm not too young to be President."

Stan was a wonderful guy. You know, here's a guy with a lifetime average of .340, I guess, at the time. You would have thought he was a .200 hitter. He just acted just as nice and sweet and humble as you'd want him to be.

A Poem from High School

Poetry has been my second love, next to baseball. My tenth grade English teacher was about to flunk me, and it was a major subject, so if she did, I couldn't play on the baseball team. After much pleading and begging on my part, she said, "Well, I'll tell you what I'll do for this report card. Write a poem, and I will grade it, but then in the next grading period and the one after that you'll bear down and do your English work." That almost scared me to death, the thought of writing a poem. I think I had about four days to do it. But I did write one, and she liked it. In fact, I wrote about the only thing I could write about, baseball. Miss Ryan gave me an A on the poem and my English did improve.

The Championship

Our centerfielder's name was Bob,
Our left was kinda fat.
Jerry was in the pitcher's box,
JW behind the bat.

We took the field without a word,
And grim was every face,
With Ray at third, Lou at first,
And John at second base.

The right fielder was big and strong,
And Mike was playing short.
We played Fremont for the championship,
Did they think they were smart!

Until against an azure sky,
Arose a mighty shout.
'Twas Ray who caught the arching fly,
And put their last man out.

And still where gallant deeds are done,
I tell this tale anew.
Our rival's score was only one,
And we came up with two.

Bill Renna

Six years (1953-56, 58-59)
Born Oct. 14, 1924 BR TR 6'3" 218 lbs.
Position: Outfield
New York Yankees, Philadelphia Athletics,
Kansas City Athletics, Boston Red Sox

G	BA	AB	H	2B	3B	HR	R	RBI	BB	SO	SB	FA
370	.239	918	219	36	10	28	123	119	99	166	2	.979

*A*s a Yankee rookie in 1953, Renna hit .314 in 61 games, sharing outfield chores with Mantle, Bauer, Woodling, and Noren. In December of 1953 he was part of the 10-player trade with the Philadelphia Athletics that brought Eddie Robinson, Loren Babe, Tom Hamilton, and Carmen Mauro to the Yankees for Don Bollweg, John Gray, Jim Robertson, Jim Finigan, Vic Power, and Renna. Renna played in 123 games and hit 13 home runs for the Athletics in 1954. In 1955 he played in 100 games for the Athletics. He started his minor league career in 1949 with Twin Falls of the Pioneer League, where he batted .385, drove in 99 runs, and hit a league-leading 21 home runs. In 1951, he led the Three-I League with 26 home runs with Quincy. In 1952, he hit 28 home runs for Kansas City in the American Association.*

Casey Stengel, Utilizing Talents

Stengel was a lot smarter than a lot of people thought. He double talked and he did these and those and all that stuff, but he was very much aware of the talents that he had. He knew how to utilize them. In fact, that was really one of his big attributes, I think, the fact that he could use the different people in the areas that they really were much better. He platooned a lot of people. They didn't like it, but they ended up on pennant winners.

He wasn't hard to play for. He didn't scream and holler. He just sat back, and he had his coaches. But he would get up and yell once in awhile. But a very good manager. He knew how to handle people. That was one of the reasons he was so successful.

Crazy Bounces at Fenway

Left field is a tough field to play because of that big tall fence, and it's metal. It's like tin, only it's thin metal, then it has the braces behind it, and if it hits the metal it'll come down dead, straight down. If it hits right in front of one of those braces in back of that fence, it will bounce differently. So the best thing to do is just stay back.

When you see it's going to hit the wall, you just turn around and run toward the infield and turn back and wait for the ball to hit, and then, whichever way it goes, field it. You just hope it doesn't hit just above that little scoreboard because then you don't know which way it's going to go.

Carl Scheib

Eleven years (1943-45, 47-54)
Born Jan. 1, 1927 BR TR 6'1" 192 lbs.
Position: Pitcher; OF, 2
Philadelphia Athletics, St. Louis Cardinals

G	W	L	PCT	ERA	GS	CG	SV	IP	H	BB	SO	BA	FA
267	45	65	.409	4.88	107	47	17	1071.2	1130	496	290	.250	.966

Signed out of high school, Scheib was the youngest player to ever appear in an AL game (16 years, eight months, five days) when he made his pro debut in 1943. He went 14-8 with a 3.84 ERA in 1948 and batted .298 (31 for 104). He went 11-7 in 1952. One of baseball's best hitting pitchers of his era, he had 57 official at-bats as a pinch-hitter. In 1951 he hit .396 (21-53).

Tryout at 15

I came from a little country town, and some grocery salesman who knew the Macks had come and seen me play some high school baseball. He arranged for a tryout when I was 15 years old.

I went down to Philadelphia one day. They were supposed to play Washington, but they were rained out. We went down to the bullpen and they had me throw a little bit. Some of the coaches were there, and of course Connie was there.

He said, "You go back to school and get down here next year as fast as you can." Being from a little country town of coal miners and farmers, nobody ever went anyplace. So I quit school and joined the Athletics when they came back from spring training. I just stayed around pitching batting practice for several months. I was with the ballclub quite a while before I signed a contract, just pitching batting practice. I'd started even making road trips with them.

We were coming home one day, and Mr. Mack was in his little room at the end of the car. He called me in and kind of hinted, "Don't you think it's about time?"

I said, "Yeah, I'm ready."

He said, "Well, have your parents come down."

They came down the next day and went up in the office and we signed a contract.

Gentleman Connie Mack

Connie Mack was a gentleman. Of course, he was getting pretty old then. A little bit on the forgetful side as far as remembering names of players. He'd want somebody to pinch hit and say, "I want, I want . . ." And he couldn't think of his name, and then one of the players would say, "You want so and so?"

"Yeah, yeah, yeah."

I bumped into him after I'd been with the club five or six years. He came down in the elevator and said, "Haven't I seen you someplace before?"

He never came in the clubhouse. The only time you saw him was at a ballgame or on the train. But he knew his baseball. You could tell that, even though he was in his later years. And he was such a gentleman, always out there in his straight collar.

Eddie Stanky

Eddie Stanky counted everything. I think he counted pitches. He timed everything. He timed how fast you ran to first base. He fined everything possible. If a guy didn't sacrifice a guy home from third on a long fly, he was fined. If he didn't bunt him over, he was fined. If a man on the bench missed a sign during the inning, he was fined. You'd just worry about all those things instead of keeping your mind in the game.

Bob Shaw

Eleven years (1957-67)

Born June 29, 33 BR TR 6'2" 195 lbs.

Position: Pitcher

Detroit Tigers, Chicago White Sox, Kansas City Athletics,
Milwaukee Braves, San Francisco Giants,
New York Mets, Chicago Cubs

G	W	L	PCT	ERA	GS	CG	SV	IP	H	BB	SO	BA	FA
430	108	98	.524	3.52	223	55	32	1778	1837	511	880	.133	.945

An All-Star in 1962, Shaw went 15-9 with the Braves with a 2.80 ERA. He pitched the last two innings of the All-Star Game to preserve a 3-1 NL win. He led the AL in winning percentage in 1959, going 18-6 for the pennant-winning White Sox. He finished second in ERA and third in the Cy Young balloting. He was 1-1 in the World Series, beating Koufax 1-0 in Game 5. In 1965 he was 16-9 for the Giants with a 2.64 ERA. He was traded to the White Sox in 1958 with Ray Boone for Bill Fischer and Tito Francona. In 1961 he was traded with Wes Covington, Gerry Staley, and Stan Johnson for Ray Herbert, Don Larsen, Andy Carey, and Al Pilarcik. In 1961 Shaw was traded with Lou Klimchock to the Braves for Joe Azcue, Ed Charles, and Manny

Jimenez. In 1963 he was traded to the Giants with Del Crandall and Bob Hendley for Billy Hoeft, Ed Bailey, and Ernie Bowman.

Teaching the Spitball

In the book that he wrote, *The Spitter and I,* do you know who Gaylord Perry said taught him the spitter? It was me. He threw a lot of them. And he will admit that. Would he throw 20 in a game, or 15 in a game? Yeah.

I made good use of the spitter at the end of my career. The techniques of the spitter? Prepare, pucker, and pop. Three P's. You have to prepare. You use a lozenge, put it under your tongue. Slippery elm lozenge. In those days you would take your glove off and I would spit it in the palm of my hand and then rub it in the ball where it says Reich. On one of the four sides where the wide part is, there's always an emblem, on every ball. So you prepare that spot. You have to prepare the ball. Most people don't know what they're doing, that's why very few guys threw the spitter. Drysdale did, Ford did, Jack Hamilton, Burdette. But there really were very, very few—because most of them didn't know what they were doing. You have to know. You put it on the ball where it's prepared, but you pucker your fingers, and then you've got to really pop your wrist. The thumb is dry and the fingers are wet, and it's coming off the leather so the ball slips out in reverse. There's only one other guy I taught the spitball to and he won 24 games that year. Tony Cloninger, remember when he won 24 games. He came up to my house and asked me to show him. *[Cloninger went 24-11 for the Braves in 1965.]*

Bob Shaw

Pitching in the '59 World Series

I lost the second game in the '59 Series 4-3 when the White Sox played the Dodgers, but then I came back and beat Koufax 1 to 0 in the Coliseum. And that was the largest crowd to ever see a World Series game—92,507. One thing that stands out is that in the 1-0 game Gil Hodges hit a ball with a man on about an inch foul, hit it a ton, and if it was fair I would have lost 2-1, but as you know, it's a game of inches. It worked out good for me.

Larry Sherry

Eleven years (1958-68)

Born July 25, 1935 BR TR 6'2" 180 lbs.

Position: Pitcher

Los Angeles Dodgers, Detroit Tigers,

Houston Astros, California Angels

G	W	L	PCT	ERA	GS	CG	SV	IP	H	BB	SO	BA	FA
416	53	44	.546	3.67	16	2	82	799.1	747	374	606	.169	.927

Called up to the big leagues in July 4, 1959, Sherry finished second to Willie McCovey in the Rookie of the Year balloting in 1959, then beat the Milwaukee Braves in the first play-off game to help the Dodgers into the World Series. He was the World Series MVP, winning two games and saving two, becoming the first pitcher to win or save all four of his team's games. He allowed only one run in 12²/₃ innings of work in the series. He also went 2-4 as a hitter in the series. Including the World Series, he won his last nine games that year, losing only two, had three saves, batted seven for 32 with two home runs, and had an ERA of 2.19. In 1960, Sherry led the National League with 13 relief wins; he also saved seven games. After his rookie year, he was almost exclusively a reliever, starting only seven games in his last nine seasons. Forty-seven of his 53 big-league wins came in relief. From 1959-1962 he and his brother

Larry Sherry

Norm, a reserve catcher, formed a brother battery with the Dodgers. After his career, he worked with both the Dodgers and Pittsburgh as a minor league coach and pitching instructor.

'59 N.L. Playoff

The World Series in 1959 when I was voted MVP is probably what I'm most remembered for. But actually the game that I think meant the most and probably did the most for the team was the first playoff game. We finished the season tied and we went into Milwaukee to play them. They had a good hitting ballclub. I relieved Danny McDevitt in the second inning, I think. I pitched seven and two-thirds innings and shut them out and got the win. It was an overcast, late September day, drizzling. It was not a day you'd want to say, "Well, let's go out and play." The field wasn't muddy, but it was starting to get wet. It was probably the most important game of the season for me and the Dodgers, so I kind of put a lot of stock in that game.

I think they thought about starting me in the game, but I hadn't started in the last month. Either because of the line-up or whatever, they decided to go with McDevitt. He was a lefthanded pitcher. I think Roseboro hit a home run in the sixth or seventh inning and we won 3-2. But I think the reason I kept pitching to the end of the ballgame against a very strong club was I was getting the job done. So that's a very memorable moment. Then there was a second playoff game and we won that one at home to go into the World Series.

The Coliseum Noise

In the 1959 Series we played in the Coliseum in Los Angeles, which was not set up for baseball, and in the three games at home we had over 270,000 people; we averaged over 92,000 a game. The noise on the floor of the Coliseum was unbelievable, especially to me, coming in relief. You couldn't hear anyone yelling or talking. We had to use hand signs because you yell for the ball on a fly ball, and the noise bounces off both sides of the stadium on the floor there. Deafening. I never heard that again, never had that kind of experience, getting the last guy out and hearing that ovation, and it being that deafening. You're struck a little bit, in awe, that it could be that loud. Nothing compares to that noise.

[Sherry was the MVP of the 1959 World Series, saving Games 2 and 3, and winning Games 4 and 6.]

Sandy Koufax

I saw Koufax after the '66 season. He told me he was going to retire. He'd had a real tough year physically; his arm was bothering him, but everybody said, "How can you throw a no-hitter and strike out so many guys and have your arm bother you?" But his arm was bothering him in the elbow, and he didn't know if he wanted to go through another season with all the amount of medication he was taking. Nobody thought he would do it, but he just up and retired.

[In 1966, Koufax' last season, he was 30 years old. He won 27, lost nine, struck out 317 batters, and had an ERA of 1.73 in 323 innings. He led the league in wins, ERA, starts, complete games, innings pitched, strikeouts, and shutouts. He won the Cy Young Award in three of his final four seasons.]

Norm Sherry

My brother and I worked together three years—Norm was a catcher. It was special being able to pitch to him. We grew up together and I used to tag along. He was four years older. He was a pretty good pull hitter, so he hit some home runs over the short porch in the Colosseum. *[Norm Sherry hit 18 home runs in his 497 major league at-bats.]*

He knew me inside and out. When he caught me, I knew what he was going to call. He taught me quite a bit. So that was a great experience, he was an awfully good receiver. In fact Koufax gave Norm a lot of credit in helping him turn it around in '61. I didn't realize at the time how sort of special that was, having my brother on the same team.

In 1959 I got called back up in July. Norm got called back in September and we were there the last month, though Roseboro was doing most of the catching. But he was there, and that was a help to me.

I recall coming in after the game that I won in Milwaukee, the playoff game, and doing, I think, a radio interview with Scully, then when I got in the clubhouse, the writers rushed to me, but they'd all been in talking to him. I looked over and there were still about half a dozen or so writers around him. Where could you get better information than from the guy's brother?

Charlie Silvera

Ten years (1948-57)

Born October 13, 1924   BR   TR   5'10"   175 lbs.

Position: Catcher

New York Yankees, Chicago Cubs

G	BA	AB	H	2B	3B	HR	R	RBI	BB	SO	SB	FA
227	.282	482	136	15	2	1	34	52	53	32	2	.985

In his first two seasons with the Yankees, Charlie batted .340 in 62 games. He hit .291 in his seven seasons with the Yankees as back-up to Yogi Berra. He caught 20 games in 1952, hitting .327 and fielding 1.000. He was one of only eight players to play on all five of the consecutive World Championship teams, 1949-53. He played in one of the 42 World Series games for which he was eligible. In 1948 Charlie caught 144 games for Portland in the Pacific Coast League, batting .301 with 85 RBIs.

Rule Changes

I was involved in two rule changes. The first was the rule that prevents a runner from going out of the base line to break up a double play. We were in Philadelphia. Nellie Fox was playing second base for the A's at that time. I hit a ball, not a sharp hit ball, but I didn't run very well, and anyway Lindell was on first. The ball was thrown to Fox, and he came off the bag and Lindell went after him and knocked him halfway into left field, let's put it that way. And he held onto the ball, and I ended up getting to first base. And the runners on second and third scored, so I got two RBIs. And the rule was changed after that.

The other rule was the one that took photographers off the playing field. There was a pop fly in Cleveland that I went after. Hegan was the hitter. Photographers were on the field, and they started running when I went over to catch the ball and I took my eye off the ball and missed it.

That's when put the rule in that took the photographers off the field.

Both rule changes were in 1949.

Sibbi Sisti

Thirteen years (1939-42, 46-54)
Born July 26, 1920 BR TR 5'11" 175 lbs.
Positions: 2B, 359; 3B, 290; SS, 179; OF, 74; 1B, 2
Boston Braves, Milwaukee Braves

G	BA	AB	H	2B	3B	HR	R	RBI	BB	SO	SB	FA
1016	.244	2999	732	121	19	27	401	260	283	440	30	.952

Sisti was the Braves' regular third baseman and second baseman from 1940-42 before going into the military. In 1946 he hit .343 with Indianapolis and was named Minor League Player of the Year by The Sporting News. *After his return to the majors he was one of the National League's best utility players. He was called "Super Sub," playing seven positions during his career with the Braves. He played in 83 games in the Braves' 1948 pennant-winning season. In 1951, he hit .279 in 114 games. He once beat out three bunt singles in a game. Sisti was a manager in the minor leagues.*

Milwaukee Fans

The Braves drew very poorly in that last year in Boston, 1952. In fact, I think the figures were like 283,000 people for the season. From what I remember, the largest crowd we had all year was about 10 to 12,000, and that was against Brooklyn, who won the pennant that year.

Then we went to Milwaukee and with practically the same ballclub, but with maybe one or two new players, and we drew more than a million people that first year. The smallest crowd we had that year was either 10 or 12,000 thousand people. That was against Pittsburgh, which was a second division ballclub, and it was a drizzly, rainy night.

That Boston Braves ballpark had a capacity seating of about 40-, 41,000, and when you get 2, 3, or 4,000 people in a stadium that size, it looked like there was nobody out there. So then when we went into Milwaukee it was like a packed house almost every game we played, so that helped charge the guys up a little more.

Ernie Lombardi

Ernie Lombardi was a tremendous hitter, a guy that couldn't run a lick. I always felt sorry for him because when I—or any infielder—played against him they would play deep on the grass, in the outfield, 'cause poor Ernie couldn't run worth a lick. And then in '42 when he came to play with the Braves I saw the same thing that I had seen three years previous, that the opposition would always play him deep. The poor guy— he hit around .300, and with ordinary speed it would have been about .350. *[Lombardi, a catcher, played 17 years, hit .306 with 190 home runs and was elected to the Hall of Fame in 1986. In 1942, his only year with the Braves, he led the league in hitting with a .330 average.]*

Sibbi Sisti

Lou Sleater

Seven years (1950-52, 55-58)

Born Sept. 8, 1926 BL TL 5'10" 185 lbs.

Position: Pitcher

St. Louis Browns, Washington Senators, Kansas City Athletics,
Milwaukee Braves, Detroit Tigers, Baltimore Orioles

G	W	L	PCT	ERA	GS	CG	SV	IP	H	BB	SO	BA	FA
131	12	18	.400	4.70	21	7	5	300.2	306	172	152	204	.906

A good hitting pitcher, Sleater hit 5-10 for the Braves in 1956 and hit three home runs in just 20 at-bats in 1957. A starter early in his career, he was used as a relief pitcher in his last four seasons with only two of his 94 appearances as a starting pitcher. In 1952 with the Senators he gave up Walt Dropo's record-tying 12th straight hit, then retired him in his next at-bat to break the streak. In 1951 Sleater was traded with Bobb Houge, Kermit Wahl, and Tom Upton to the Yankees for Cliff Mapes. In 1952, he was traded with Freddie Marsh to the Senators from the Browns for Cass Michaels. In addition to his six big-league clubs, he pitched for 12 different minor league teams, three times winning 12 or more games.

Dropo's Twelve Straight Hits

In July 1952, I was on the Washington Senators' pitching staff when the Detroit Tigers came to town. The Tigers' Walt Dropo had just got a bunch of consecutive hits in a doubleheader against the Yankees in New York the day before. We played them in a twilight doubleheader, and Dropo was still red hot. He continued his streak of consecutive hits into the second game. I came into the second game in relief of Bob Porterfield.

In the middle of the game, Walt tied the consecutive hit record off me with his 12th straight hit. The record had been set in 1938 by Mike "Pinky" Higgins of the Boston Red Sox. The next time at bat against me, going for the record 13th straight hit, he popped up a fast ball to the catcher, Mickey Grasso.

Several years ago I went to the Hall of Fame in Cooperstown, New York, to be with Walt, his brother George, and many of his friends, when he presented the ball from his record-tying hit to the Hall of Fame.

The No-Hitter

The no-hitter was within reach. All I had to do in the ninth was retire Peanuts Lowry, Red Schoendienst, Stan (the Man) Musial. Lowry grounded out. Schoendienst popped to short. Musial took a ball and a strike, then grounded out to second base.

Why isn't it in the record books? Did I only dream it, wish it were so?

No, it happened, but in spring training, 1951, Browns vs. Cardinals, in Houston. Ned Garver pitched eight innings, left for a pinch hitter, Johnny Bero. He drove in the game's only run and rookie Lou Sleater came in to pitch.

Lowry, Schoendienst, Musial. What a trio.

I can't help but wonder—was there ever another time in his career that Stan the Man was the final out in a no-hitter?

Elvin Tappe

Six years (1954-56, 58, 60, 62)

Born May 21, 1927 BR TR 5'11" 180 lbs.

Position: Catcher

Chicago Cubs

G	BA	AB	H	2B	3B	HR	R	RBI	BB	SO	SB	FA
145	.207	304	63	10	0	0	21	17	29	25	0	.989

El was one of the rotating managers in the Cubs' College of Coaches experiment during the 1961-62 seasons. A fine defensive catcher, he saw greatest amount of playing time in his rookie year (1954), playing in 46 games behind Garagiola and Walker Cooper; and in 1960, playing in 51 games while splitting catching duties with Moe Thacker and Earl Averill.

The Cubs' Rotating Coaches

It was my idea, the rotating coaches. I just felt that we were making too many changes, and instead of rotating managers all the time and bringing in more coaches, if we could systemize the thing and have the same system of play, if you were compelled to have a new manager, you wouldn't have to replace all the coaches. Let your coaches be organizational people.

We had a bunch of great arms back in those days with Drott and Drabowski and Hobie and Ellsworth. I just felt that every time we made a managerial change they would have to bring in a new pitching coach, and pitching is 95 percent of it, and I just felt we were hurting those young arms.

And what we were doing is what everybody is doing now. I mean, everybody is having minor league pitching instructors and minor league hitting instructors and everything like that. We were more or less the pioneers of that. I didn't really cater to Mr. Wrigley's idea of rotating the manager; all I wanted to do was rotate the coaches.

The press didn't accept it. The players didn't accept it. The press want to have one guy they can get on. And really, it presented an alibi to the players, and any time you can present an alibi to the players they'll use it. They always said they didn't know who was in charge. But really, in any athletic contest you have to go out there and do the job. No matter who's in charge, who's on the bench, that doesn't matter.

The press just crucified us with it. But everybody now is going to the rotating coaching system, as far as rotating their coaches in the minor leagues. That was my intent. To get instruction at the minor league level.

But Mr. Wrigley, he went all the way, rotating the managers and everything. Which was his prerogative, he owned the ballclub, he could do what he wanted to.

Ernie Banks

Ernie was just the salt of the earth. You talk about a real class act, he really was. I mean, he was always friendly, he always had time for the fans. He always had time for the kids to sign autographs. I can remember him sitting there maybe an hour after the game, just sitting on the bench outside the park signing autographs for kids. He'd have pictures taken, they'd sit on his lap. I mean, you talk about a real classy person, Ernie was.

Wayne Terwilliger

Nine years (1949-51, 53-56, 59-60)

Born June 27, 1925   BR   TR   5'11"   165 lbs.

Positions: 2B, 605; 3B, 14; SS, 6; 1B, 1; OF, 1

Chicago Cubs, Brooklyn Dodgers, Washington Senators,
New York Giants, Kansas City Athletics

G	BA	AB	H	2B	3B	HR	R	RBI	BB	SO	SB	FA
666	.240	2091	501	93	10	22	271	162	247	296	31	.974

In his rookie year with the Cubs, Terwilliger got eight consecutive hits. He was part of the eight-player Cubs-Dodgers trade in 1951, going to Brooklyn with Pafko, Johnny Schmitz, and Rube Walker for Bruce Edwards, Joe Hatten, Eddie Miksis, and Gene Hermanski. A star shortstop in college at Western Michigan University, he played mainly second base in the big leagues, including three seasons as a regular, one with the Cubs and two with the Senators. Terwilliger is a lifelong baseball man, coached for several big-league teams, including four years for Ted Williams at Washington and Texas. His highest batting average in the majors was in 1959 when he hit .267 in 74 games with the Athletics.

From the Cubs to the Dodgers

The first time I was traded was when I was with the Cubs in 1951. I was sitting in the john in our apartment in Chicago and had the radio going, and I heard the trade announced. They said, "A big trade today, the Cubs and Dodgers." And they started naming them off. *[Terwilliger was traded to the Dodgers with Andy Pafko, Johnny Schmitz, and Rube Walker for Bruce Edwards, Joe Hatten, Eddie Miksis, and Gene Hermanski.]* I think I was the last one named off, and I couldn't believe it. That's the way I found out. The Dodgers were in town that day, so I went to the ballpark. There was no big deal or anything. I don't remember anybody saying anything to me.

I got my gear together and walked over to the Dodger locker room, put my stuff in there. And I didn't like it. Because I thought, "Holy smokes, here I am in the big leagues finally, and I know some guys on the club, and now I'm with a club where I know nobody."

Pee Wee Reese was great. When we got back to Brooklyn, I found a place to live. Reese said, "You tell me where you are and I'll come over and pick you up and take you to the park the first day. Get you straightened around." And he did that. He took me to the park the first day and showed me the way to go. I remember, he and Hodges were great, right off the bat. The bigger the star, the bigger the person was, I thought. They were a bunch of good guys, the Dodgers.

Manager Ted Williams

I got a chance to coach for Ted when he managed the Senators. I can recall him saying, "You got to have enthusiasm, you've got to be enthusiastic in this game." And that's what he believed. And he was great.

I know he enjoyed his first couple years as a manager, because he used to sit in the dugout in the back and he'd bring in a lefthanded pitcher named Dennis Riddleberger—I'll never forget him *[Riddleberger pitched from 1970-72. In 103 games, all in relief, he won four, lost four, and saved one, with an ERA of 2.77]*—to face Boog Powell. He did that three or four times and Riddleberger threw that slow stuff up there and big Powell he would swing from his butt, you know, and couldn't hit it, and Williams used to get in the corner of the dugout and laugh until tears came out of his eyes.

Frank Thomas

Sixteen years (1951-66)

Born June 11, 1929   BR   TR   6'3"   200 lbs.

Positions: OF, 1045; 3B, 394; 1B, 271; 2B, 4

Pittsburgh Pirates, Cincinnati Reds, Chicago Cubs, Milwaukee Braves,
New York Mets, Philadelphia Phillies, Houston Astros

G	BA	AB	H	2B	3B	HR	R	RBI	BB	SO	SB	FA
1766	.266	6285	1671	262	31	286	792	962	484	894	15	.971

*Thomas was a three-time All-Star. From 1953-62 he hit
20 or more home runs nine times; he hit 30 or more
three times. Twice he drove in over 100 runs. In 1954 he hit .298
in 153 games for Pittsburgh, with 23 home runs and 93 RBIs. In
1958 he hit 35 home runs with 109 RBIs for Pittsburgh. He was
involved in a 1959 trade with the Reds that sent Burgess, Haddix,
and Hoak to the Pirates. Thomas hit 34 home runs for the 1962
Mets team that lost 120 games. In that season he hit two homers in
each of three consecutive games. In the minor leagues, he twice led
his league in rbi (132 in 1948 and 131 in 1952). He hit a total of
100 minor league home runs.*

The Gynecologist and the Thumb

I think 1958 had to be my favorite season because I had a great year. It just so happened that I got hurt on September 3. I had 32 home runs at that time and I only hit three more home runs the rest of the year because I had a bad thumb. Tom Acker hit me with a pitch real close to where the bat had broken and wedged into my thumb. After the season was over I had it operated on. A gynecologist operated on my thumb. He was the team doctor, but gynecology was what he specialized in.

About a month and a half after he operated I said, "You didn't get what was in there, it's still there."

He said, "Oh, that'll go away."

Then I got traded. I got traded from Pittsburgh to Cincinnati with a bad hand, but no one would believe me. I hit 12 home runs the next season. You don't go from 35 home runs to 12 when you're in the prime of your career unless there's something radically wrong. After the '59 season the Cubs were interested in me so they wanted their doctor to see me. He took X-rays, and then he operated on me.

After I came out of the anesthesia, he said, "I think there's going to be a lot of red faces."

I said, "What do you mean?"

He said, "Well, I don't know how you hit 12 home runs with the type of hand that you had."

I had tumors going around my nerve. You know how it feels you drink cold water on a tooth? The nerve? Well, that's the way it was when I picked up a bat. I had tears in my eyes. I did everything, but I never asked to get taken out of the line-up. If my name was put in the line-up I went out and I played. I put a doughnut on the bat, put tape around my hand, I did everything. But it was just one of those unfortunate things.

After I had the operation, I hit 21 home runs. Then I hit 27 home runs the following year, and I hit 34 home runs the next year, so that was kind of proof that something was wrong.

Frank Thomas

Good Medicine

In 1964 when I was with the Mets I was in the hospital for 41 days. When I got out of the hospital I went to the ballpark, and Casey asked me if I could pinch hit in the last of the ninth inning against the Cardinals. Curt Simmons was pitching, a lefthanded pitcher. I got the count to three and two and hit the next pitch out of the ballpark for a home run. Coming out of the hospital and being able to do something like that was probably the most dramatic moment of my career.

John Holland

Out of all the general managers that I dealt with, I would say that John Holland of the Cubs was one who would listen to you. A good example of that is in 1960 when I was with the Cubs. We were in Pittsburgh and Boudreau was the manager. I was second to Banks in home runs, and one day I'm not in the line-up. They brought up Santo [*a third baseman*] and they brought up this kid Murphy [*Danny—hit .120 in 31 games for the Cubs that year*] who they gave a $125,000 to—an outfielder. I went to Lou and I said, "What does this mean, Lou?"

He said, "You're just going to be playing against lefthanded pitching."

I said, "Whose idea is this?"

He said, "It's mine."

I was the type of player who would root for the player that was in there, but I didn't do that this time. They went out and pitched batting practice and I sat in the corner and I pouted like a little kid. I knew this would get to Boudreau. I just stayed that way until we got to L.A. Then he put me into pinch hit against Drysdale.

After the game he asked me when I was going to have breakfast the next day. He told me, "How about coming down a little early? John Holland and I want to talk to you."

So I came down early. After the waitress took our order he asked, "What seems to be the problem?"

I said, "There's no problem, John. All I want to do is play. I'm second to Banks in home runs and I can't play on this club?"

Well, he threw a check on the table for a $1000, and he said, "If your attitude changes, I'll double that at the end of the year."

I said, "John, you're not going to buy me. I don't want that. I signed a contract to do whatever you want me to do, but not the way it was done."

He said, "Well, give it to your wife."

I said, "No, I don't want it." So then he shoved it in my pocket, and then two weeks before the season was over he called me up to his office. He gave me another check for $2,000.

I said, "John, if I get a contract this year and you cut my salary I'm going to give you the $3,000 back and I'm going to let you know about it."

Sure enough, they cut my salary $8,000. I wrote him a 10-page letter. As soon as he got the letter, he got on the phone and said, "I want you to fly into Chicago."

I flew into Chicago, he sat me down, and he said, "I got your letter."

I said, "Well, what do you think? Put yourself in my shoes."

He said, "I'd feel the same way." He said, "I'll tell you what. I'll take the $3,000 back and I won't cut your salary."

I said, "Fine." He was a straight-shooter and I really enjoyed my dealings with him. *[Thomas finished the year second on the Cubs in home runs and runs batted in.]*

Tying a Record

In 1962, I hit six home runs in three consecutive games. They came against Philadelphia. I remember that Art Mahaffey and Turk Farrell were two of the pitchers. It tied a record with six or seven guys. *[Other players to do it are Ralph Kiner, Gus Zernial, Tony Lazzeri, Frank Howard, Lee May, and Mike Schmidt.]* I had a chance to break it the next day. We played a doubleheader against Cincinnati. In the first game I hit one that just went foul. In the second game I hit one in the 14th inning that won the game. If the one in the first game had stayed fair, it'd have been seven in four games and then eight in five games. *[Frank Howard is the only player to have eight home runs in five consecutive games with at least one home run in each game.]*

Bobby Thomson

Fifteen years (1946-60)

Born Oct. 25, 1923 BR TR 6'2" 180 lbs.

Positions: Outfield, 1506; 3B, 184; 2B, 9; 1B, 1

New York Giants, Milwaukee Braves, Chicago Cubs,

Boston Red Sox, Baltimore Orioles

G	BA	AB	H	2B	3B	HR	R	RBI	BB	SO	SB	FA
1779	.270	6305	1705	267	74	264	903	1026	559	804	38	.973

A *three-time All-Star, Thomson hit perhaps the most famous home run in baseball history on October 3, 1951: the three-run homer off Ralph Branca ended the National League season, giving the Giants a dramatic playoff victory over the Dodgers and the NL pennant. He hit 20 or more home runs eight times. He had four 100+ RBI seasons. He hit 32 home runs in the Giants' 1951 pennant-winning season. His switch to third base that year allowed Willie Mays to take over in center field. He was traded to Milwaukee in 1954 with Sammy Calderone for Johnny Antonelli, Don Liddle, Ebba St. Claire, and Billy Klaus. In 1957, he was traded back to the Giants with Danny O'Connell and Ray Crone for Red Schoendienst. He was born in Scotland.*

No Storybook Ending This Time

Probably the biggest disappointment of my life was when I played with the Braves and we lost out for the pennant in the last weekend. We were playing in St. Louis and we were losing. There was a big run on second base and I came up and I didn't get it in, and that hurt.

But I guess I was always the guy up there hitting the home run. I guess people always expected it.

Just Playing Is Incentive Enough

When there were 60,000 people in the stands, that generates excitement. But if there are only 3,500 people in the stands and you're playing for Mr. Durocher, when that first ball is hit—I played center field before Willie—and boy, I better go get that ball, whether there are 3,000 fans or the park was full.

I always loved playing weekends in Chicago, because I always thought the Chicago fans were great. Boy, the park would be filled, and they'd always have a huge band way up behind home plate, in the upper deck. It was just wonderful. I always felt so relaxed, and I couldn't believe they were paying me to have fun like that. I wasn't trying any harder then than some other place, but there's always great incentive playing before a crowd like that.

Although we didn't need incentive, because just putting on our suits was enough incentive.

Bobby Thomson

Virgil Trucks

Seventeen years (1941-43, 45-58)

Born April 26, 1919 BR TR 5'11" 198 lbs.

Position: Pitcher

Detroit Tigers, St. Louis Browns, Chicago White Sox,
Kansas City Athletics, New York Yankees

G	W	L	PCT	ERA	GS	CG	SV	IP	H	BB	SO	BA	FA
517	177	135	.567	3.39	328	124	30	2682.1	2416	1088	1534	.180	.955

*T*rucks pitched 35 career shutouts, 72nd on the all-time
list. He is one of only four pitchers to pitch two no-hitters
in a single season (1952); he won both 1-0. Ten times he won 10 or
more games in a season. He had a complete game win in the 1945
World Series, after pitching in only one regular-season game (without a decision), making him the only pitcher to win a World Series
game after not winning a game during the regular season. A two-
time All-Star, he won 20 games in 1953 and 19 in 1949 and 1954.
In the minor leagues, he won 65 games and had four no-hitters. In
1938, Trucks' first minor league season (at age 19), pitching in
Andalusia in the Alabama-Florida League, he went 26-5 with a
1.25 ERA. His 418 strikeouts—in 273 innings—are the second
highest total in the history of professional ball.

Barnstorming

In the years that we played, like in the '30s, '40s, and even '50s, television wasn't so predominate, so the ballplayers would go on barnstorming tours after the season was over to make enough money to live off that winter. You'd go in little towns and you'd play the local towns and you'd make maybe $100 a night.

Actually, when the tour was over you probably had more money than you made all season just playing them, because in those years the owners, the companies, would not hire a baseball player, because they knew when spring came he had to hire somebody else and retrain him all over again. So we made enough money out of barnstorming to survive for the winter until we got our contract for the next year.

Barnstorming was really a great thing, it was good for baseball, it was good for the players, it was good for the fans because you played in little towns of three, four thousand population, but you'd fill up the ballpark, and you'd get paid to do that. If we didn't have barnstorming, I don't know how we could have made it through the winter.

The ballclubs wouldn't allow you to have more than any three players off of any team. So for instance, we'd have three Detroit players, three White Sox players, three Yankee players, or three of the National League. It didn't matter where you got the players. And you usually only took 12 players because that cut down on the expenses. We traveled by car, with three or four players to a car. We'd go from town—we played just like one-night stands. Every night we were playing in some little ballpark like a couple hundred, 300 miles apart.

It was great for us. We enjoyed it. We got to meet and know a lot of the National League players that way. Some players we would have never met in the National League had we not gone on these barnstorming tours.

A Hundred Miles an Hour

We were all clocked by an old Army gun. Feller and I and Atley Donald, who played for the New York Yankees. *[Donald pitched for the Yankees eight seasons, winning 65, losing 33.]* I was clocked at a hundred and five. Donald was clocked even higher than that. Feller was clocked at a 102. There were only a handful of guys at that time that could throw the ball over a 100 miles an hour. Consistently, Feller and I were the only two at that time that threw almost every pitch 100 m.p.h. or better.

In fact, I have a picture on my wall signed by Ted Williams that says, "If they say the ballplayers throw a hundred miles an hour today, you threw a hundred and ten." It's right there on the picture. And of course, he's always been one of my favorite people. He's always praised me one way or the other, but he should, he hit enough off me.

'45 Pennant Race

In 1945, I started the final game of the season, a game we had to win for the pennant. It was the only game I pitched all season. I had been in a rehabilitation camp in Norman, Oklahoma, in the Navy. And I had no way of playing ball. But I went out and worked out as much as I could by myself. There was a catcher there, a minor league baseball player, and he was at the base, we'd work out every day. He wasn't going anyplace, he was just helping me out.

So when I got to St. Louis, I pitched until the sixth inning in that last game. When I went out of the game we were winning 2–1. I guess Steve O'Neill, the manager at that time, felt he should bring in a pitcher who had been playing all year and was in better condition than I was, which was Newhouser. The Browns tied up the ballgame 2–2, and then it went on in the eighth inning and Hank

Greenberg hit a grandslam home run, which got us in the World Series.

I just got there two days before the season ended. Paul Richards was the catcher on the ballclub, and Paul went out and worked out with me; I threw some to him underneath the stands. It rained that latter part of the season; the last three games it was raining. In fact, if we had lost that ballgame that I did start, we would have had to play the second game in the rain or else it would have wound up being a tie and we would have had to play the Washington Senators a playoff ballgame back in Detroit to decide who won the pennant that year. But that didn't happen.

I guess O'Neill started me that game because at least I had played two years in the major leagues before I went in the service and had fairly successful years in the major leagues. And maybe he felt that it would be a surprise thing. In baseball in those years they did use surprise tactics. And he felt that I was a big strong guy, a young guy, and his pitching staff was pretty well depleted at that particular time. Really and frankly, if it had been me, I would have had to go to one of my veteran pitchers who had been with me all year. I would have not started me, had I been Steve O'Neill. He just had a hunch. And of course Paul Richards knew me and felt that I was capable of doing whatever O'Neill wanted me to do.

Yogi Berra

Yogi was the most uncommon hitter who ever existed. Your best bet to pitch to Yogi would be to throw the ball down the middle and forget about it. 'Cause if you threw it over his head he was liable to hit it out of the park. If you threw it down the top of his shoes, he may hit a double out of it. He was the most unorthodox good hitter I ever saw in my life.

Tom Upton

Three years (1950-52)

Born Dec. 29, 1926 BR TR 6'0" 160 lbs.

Positions: SS, 165; 2B, 2; 3B, 1

St. Louis Browns, Washington Senators

G	BA	AB	H	2B	3B	HR	R	RBI	BB	SO	SB	FA
181	.225	525	181	9	9	2	60	42	65	67	8	.948

Upton was the Browns' regular shortstop his rookie season, 1950, and hit .237 in 124 games. He handled 15 chances at shortstop in one game, only two off the American League record of 17 set by Roderick Wallace of the Browns in 1902. After he left baseball, Tom was a college math professor for 35 years.

Things to Remember

I'm sure I remember them better than they remember me—teammates like Ned Garver, 20-game winner with a last-place club; Ken Wood, best arm from right field at the time; opponents like the Yankees' DiMaggio, Mantle, Berra, Rizzuto, Reynolds, Raschi, and Ford; Boudreau of Cleveland; Bobby Doerr and Ted Williams of the Red Sox; and Bob Feller of the Indians.

A few moments stand out from those days over 40 years ago: my lead off hit against Billy Pierce on opening day; the day the Red Sox beat us, the Browns, 29-3—all we could do was watch and wonder "Will it ever end?"; the day I handled 15 chances at short-stop, only two short of the American League record. I was lucky. Even though baseball didn't pay much then it enabled me to finish my education to become a college math professor for 35 years. Yes, there is life after baseball.

Bill Virdon

Twelve years (1955-65, 68)
Born June 9, 1931   BL   TR   6'0"   175 lbs.
Position: Outfield
St. Louis Cardinals, Pittsburgh Pirates

G	BA	AB	H	2B	3B	HR	R	RBI	BB	SO	SB	FA
1583	.267	5980	1596	237	81	91	735	502	442	647	47	.982

*B*ill was signed by the Yankees and went to the Cardinals
in 1954 in the trade that sent Enos Slaughter to the Yankees. In 1954, Bill led the International League in hitting with a
.333 mark while hitting 22 home runs and driving in 98 runs for
Rochester. He was the National League Rookie of the Year in 1955,
batting .281 with a career-high 17 home runs for the Cardinals.
The following year he was traded to the Pirates after 24 games for
Dick Littlefield and Bobby Del Greco and hit .334 in his 133 games
for the Pirates. Four times Bill hit 10 or more triples in a season,
leading the league with 10 triples in 1962; he was also a Gold Glove
winner that year. In the Pirates' 1960 World Series triumph over the
Yankees, Bill sparkled in the field. It was his ground ball that took
the bad hop in Game 7 and hit Kubek in the throat, opening the
door for the key runs that made the Pirates' comeback victory pos-

sible. In 13 years as a major league manager with the Pirates, Yankees, Astros, and Expos, Bill's teams had a record of 995-921. He was twice named TSN Manager of the Year (in 1974 with the Yankees and 1980 with the Astros).

'60 World Series

I think two instances in the '60 Series that come to mind are the bad hop that hit Kubek in the throat. That really was the break we needed. After the bad hop we scored five runs. You have to think that someone was looking out after us. I hit the ball that hit Kubek in the throat, and I hit the ball well, but if it had not taken a bad hop, it was a routine double-play ball.

If it doesn't take the bad hop, we've got two outs in the eighth inning and we're down 7-4. Most instances you don't win when you get in that situation. That doesn't mean we wouldn't have won, because that club usually found a way to score some runs enough to win. But that was one of the breaks that we needed to win the Series.

In the first game of the series we were losing 1-0. Maris had hit a home run in the top of the first. But I led off the bottom of the first and I walked. Dick Groat and I hit and run a lot. He put on the hit and run sign and then took it off and I didn't see him take it off. I went on the pitch and Dick took the pitch and Yogi Berra threw the ball and nobody covered second, and I went to third and we scored three runs after that. I have to think that was a break. *[The Pirates won the game 6-4.]* So I can look back at those two instances that I was involved in that were important.

But a lot of people did the job, and I think it takes the whole 25 players to get the job done.

Bill Virdon

Lee Walls

Ten years (1952, 56-64)

Born Jan. 6, 1933   BR   TR   6'3"   205 lbs.

Positions: OF, 600; 3B, 68; 1B, 53; C, 1

Pittsburgh Pirates, Chicago Cubs, Cincinnati Reds,

Philadelphia Phillies, Los Angeles Dodgers

G	BA	AB	H	2B	3B	HR	R	RBI	BB	SO	SB	FA
902	.262	2558	670	88	31	66	331	284	245	470	21	.975

In Walls' first full big-league season, 1956, he hit .274 for the Pirates with 11 triples and 11 home runs. With the Cubs in 1957, he hit for the cycle on July 2. In 1958, he hit .304 for the Cubs with 24 home runs, including three in an August 24 game and was named to the All-Star team. In 1961 he hit .280 for the Phillies, going 13-27 as a pinch hitter. He played for the Hanku Braves in Japan in 1965-66 and later coached for the Oakland Athletics and New York Yankees. In 1985 he managed the Triple A Nashville team. In his first pro season, he hit .342 for Modesto with 14 home runs, 109 RBIs, and a league-leading 16 triples. In 1957, he was traded from the Pirates with Dale Long for Gene Baker and Dee Fondy. In 1959, the Cubs traded him to the Reds with Bill Henry and Lou Jackson for Frank Thomas. In 1960, he was included in a trade to the Phillies that returned Wally Post to Cincinnati. In 1961, he was traded to the Dodgers for Charlie Neal.

Seeing Better

I wasn't seeing the ball very well when I was with Hollywood in the Pacific Coast League. I visited an oculist who studied my glasses.

He asked, "Did you do anything to these glasses?"

I told him that I dropped them and the lenses popped out, so I put them back in."

He said, "You put them back in the wrong way."

I hit better after that.

Pinch-Hitting: The Toughest Job

Pinch hitting is the toughest job in the world. Every time they asked Snider to do it, his face got red and his hands trembled. Jerry Lynch did the same thing at Cincinnati, and I did too. It's nothing to be ashamed of. When they call on you to pinch hit, you know there's a load on your shoulders and if you have the pride I had, you want to be absolutely certain you do your best. *[Walls was the most successful pinch hitter in the majors in 1962 with the Dodgers, going 13 for 27, a .481 average].*

Playing for Mr. Wrigley

Playing in Chicago was wonderful—the fans, the park, day baseball, living a fairly normal life, being home each night. Ballplayers should have paid Mr. Wrigley to play there. Mr. Wrigley was great to play for, especially with his incentive plans. For instance, April, 1958—$1,000 per home run. I hit three home runs in one ball game against the Dodgers in the Coliseum, hit eight in all on the road trip.

When the club returned to Chicago Mr. Wrigley called me into his office. He gave me $8,000 plus $5,000 raise on my salary for the year. Mr. Wrigley, Wrigley Field, Chicago—a perfect combination for a player.

Hal White

Twelve years (1941-43, 46-54)

Born March 18, 1919 BL TR 5'10" 165 lbs.

Position: Pitcher

Detroit Tigers, St. Louis Browns, St. Louis Cardinals

G	W	L	PCT	ERA	GS	CG	SV	IP	H	BB	SO	BA	FA
336	46	54	.460	3.78	67	23	25	920.1	875	450	349	.145	.946

*W*hite went 12-12 with four shutouts and a 2.91 ERA for the Browns as a rookie in 1942. Forty-nine of his 67 big-league starts came before he left for two years of military service. When he came back from two years in the Navy, he was used mostly in relief. In his last full season, 1953, he appeared in 59 games for the Browns and Cardinals with a 6-5 record, seven saves, and a 2.94 ERA. One of his four complete games (pitched in only 18 spot starts during his nine post-World War II seasons) was a two-hit shutout for the Tigers against the Yankees in the midst of a tight pennant race on August 3, 1950. [The Tigers finished the season in second, three games back.]

Dizzy Trout

The most memorable player during my pitching career in the American League was Paul "Dizzy" Trout, who was on the pitching staff with me at Detroit. He had a heart as big at Tiger Stadium. He was a great competitor and I really looked up to him as a pitcher and a real friend. He was a very kind man to everyone and I am so proud to have been so close to him and his family over the years. Diz was my roommate for seven years at Detroit and I got to know him inside and out. He had one bad ear and it seemed like he always slept on his good ear. So who do you think had to answer the phone almost all the time? That's right, me.

'50 A.L. Pennant Race

During the pennant drive in August of 1950 during the time we *[the Detroit Tigers]* were fighting for first place against the New York Yankees, Red Rolfe, our manager, gave me a chance to start against the Yankees at Detroit. So on August 3, 1950, I pitched a complete game, allowing the Yankees two hits, and shut them out by a 4-0 score. That date I will never forget. *[White pitched six shutouts in 49 starts in the 1942-43 seasons, but started only 18 games during his next nine seasons.]*

Gene Woodling

Seventeen years (1943, 46-47, 49-62)
Born August 16, 1922 BL TR 5'9 1/2" 195 lbs.
Position: Outfield
Cleveland Indians, Pittsburgh Pirates, New York Yankees,
Baltimore Orioles, Washington Senators, New York Mets

G	BA	AB	H	2B	3B	HR	R	RBI	BB	SO	SB	FA
1796	.284	5587	1585	257	63	147	830	830	921	477	29	.989

*G*ene was an All-Star in 1959. He played on five World Championship teams with the Yankees, 1949-53. He batted .318 in 26 World Series games and is 10th on the all-time list for both World Series walks and runs scored. After the 1954 season, he was part of the 17-player trade between the Yankees and Orioles that brought Don Larsen and Bob Turley to the Yankees. In 13 big-league seasons he played in more than 100 games, batting over .300 five times. His career high in both batting, home runs, and RBIs came with Cleveland in 1957 (.321, 19, and 78). He hit 10 or more home runs nine times. A great defensive outfielder, he had only 35 career errors in over 3,000 chances. Gene won four minor league batting titles with averages of .398, .394, .344, and .385. With San Francisco of the Pacific Coast League in 1948 he *not only led the league in hitting with his .385 mark, he had 202 hits, 107 RBIs, and led the league with 13 triples. He spent two years in the Navy in World War II.*

Gold Dust Twins

Hank Bauer and I were real close friends, and we had almost identical careers; well, they called us the "Gold Dust Twins." *[Woodling played 17 years, hit .284 with 147 home runs, 830 RBIs and 830 runs; he played in five World Series. Bauer played 14 years, hit .277 with 164 home runs, 703 RBIs and 833 runs. He played in nine World Series. Bauer played from 1948-61.]*

Hank was a helluva good outfielder. He had a much stronger arm than I did. I could catch the ball. Well, in New York you damn sure better catch the ball.

We could all run. This is something the Yankee ballclub never got credit for. We never hit into ground-ball double plays. Very few. We could all run. We were a helluva defensive ballclub. Defense will always beat offense, and when you take in defense, you're taking in pitching, of course. We had Reynolds, Raschi, Lopat, and Ford. There's no better. We weren't a great hitting ballclub; we were good, but not great. But by God we didn't hit into double plays to take us out of innings and stuff. You don't win as many World Series in a row as we did if you're not a good ballclub.

Getting Ready to Play

In the winters I swam a lot. I come from a family of swimmers. I had a brother who was national champion at Ohio State.

The best conditioned athlete in the world is a swimmer. And the worst conditioned athlete is a baseball player. Swimming, you really have to train, and when you're in that pool, ain't nobody helping you. I think that's what put that drive in me. I was never nervous. I had pressure since I was a little boy, from swimming. So pressure never bothered me.

Before the game I'd go out and run some in the outfield, and then we'd take our natural infield and outfield practice. That was it. I was always good and loose when the ballgame started. Oh, I was always ready to go. I don't understand all these pulled muscles today. That tells me that their weights and this business—that's not getting in shape for baseball. I strongly don't believe in weights. A baseball player has to have a different type body from basketball or football. Baseball's a reflex game. I think running is the basic thing for baseball. For pitchers and for everybody. Running will get your body in shape for anything.

The after-game routine was very normal. I'm not going to tell you I don't drink, but I drank in moderation. Anything you overdo is going to hurt you. I'll tell you one thing. You've gotta get your sleep. I managed to do that. I didn't abuse myself.

Gus Zernial

Eleven years (1949-59)
Born June 27, 1923 BR TR 6'2 1/2" 210 lbs.
Position: Outfield (1B, 35)
Chicago White Sox, Philadelphia Athletics,
Kansas City Athletics, Detroit Tigers

G	BA	AB	H	2B	3B	HR	R	RBI	BB	SO	SB	FA
1234	.265	4131	1093	159	22	237	572	776	383	755	15	.968

An All-Star in 1953, Gus hit more home runs in the 1950s than any American Leaguer except Mantle and Berra. On October 1, 1950, he hit four home runs in a doubleheader at Comiskey Park, the only player to ever do so. In 1951, his 33 home runs and 129 RBIs led the league. That same year he hit a record-tying seven home runs over a four-game period. In 1953, his 42 home runs were just one behind Rosen's league-leading total. From 1950 to 1957, he averaged 28 home runs and 86 RBIs per season. In 1958, he had a league-leading 15 pinch hits for Detroit, hitting .395 as a pinch hitter. From 1946-48, he hit .333, .344, and .322 in the minors with 41 home runs for Burlington in the Carolina League, and with 40 home runs and 156 RBIs for Hollywood of the

Pacific Coast League. He was part of a three-club trade in 1951 that sent him to Philadelphia with Dave Philley and that sent Minoso from Cleveland to the White Sox. In 1957, Gus was traded to the Tigers with Billy Martin, Tom Morgan, Lou Skizas, Mickey McDermott, and Tim Thompson for seven players, including Bill Tuttle, Duke Maas, and Frank House.

Record Performance

In 1951, I hit seven home runs in four games. I didn't even know it was a record until I'd hit the seventh home run. We were playing in Philadelphia and I'd hit two home runs in two consecutive games and when I hit two home runs in a third consecutive game it tied a record which was set by Lazarri, I think. Of course, then they started talking about records. You know, who hit the most in three games, four games. So the day that I went out and hit the seventh home run I was well aware of the record. I think Kiner holds the record of eight home runs in four consecutive games. *[2-1-3-2]* I don't remember trying to hit an eighth home run or anything, I was just trying to hit the ball. But I was aware of the record.

Another incident that I remember more than even that is when I hit four home runs in a doubleheader in Chicago in Comiskey Park. I remember that situation because I'd hit one in the first game and I hit three in the second game, and I had a chance to hit the fourth home run if Gordon Goldsberry would have gotten on base. There was a lefthander pitching and I can't remember what his name was, but anyway I didn't get the chance, 'cause Gordie was trying to coax him out of a base on balls and I think he ended up striking out.

Celebrate the Heroes of Baseball

in These Other Acclaimed Titles from Sports Publishing!